WINE MAKING MADE EASY

HOW TO MAKE EASY HOMEMADE WINE FROM GRAPES, FRUIT, & MORE

MARY ELLEN WARD

CONTENTS

RESOURCES

DEDICATION

Though many family and friends were in the running as contenders for
the dedication of this book, due, in no small part, to their
"appreciation" of various varieties of my homemade wines, there is, at
heart, only "one who rules them all." The ruler of my heart; the co-
ruler of my home; the lover of all things wine and elderberry, my
biggest wine-making proponent (for primarily selfish reasons), the
believer in my books and in myself.
My husband...my love...
my Bill.

INTRODUCTION

In the words of my virtual "mentor" (a term used in the loosest sense as I have never actually met Frank Petersohn personally),

"If you think you know the meaning of the word Sommelier, DO NOT READ ANY FURTHER!"
(Frank Petersohn, "How to Make Wine in No Time, the Cheap Way")

All kidding aside, this is not necessarily a book for the very serious wine connoisseur. This is a book for the semi-serious home wine dabbler; the one who just wants to make good wine without risking the nest egg on a cellar full of expensive equipment. Who knows that before *chemistry*, there was wine. Good, simple, honest stuff the monks and mothers, fathers and grandfathers and others made, and enjoyed, for centuries upon centuries from what they had available to them.

Many of us have considered trying our hand at making our own homemade wine at one point or another. In theory, the idea seems doable. A few "Googling" minutes later, however, and the endeavor seems much less manageable. Deciphering winemaking books is an act in chemical frustration, and the required investment in equipment and supplies for an as-yet-unknown outcome quickly can quickly call the whole project into question.

This is the very situation I was faced with when I first considered making my own homemade wine. It was our first autumn in our new home and we were blessed with an abundance of wild grapes growing on and around the property. I knew the old monks and local old-timers once made good wines without a lot of fuss and investment, and without needing a college degree in chemistry. I had no interest in involving myself in something that required a lot of testing, balancing, additives, and fine-tune measurement. I just wanted to make a good, rustic, basic homemade wine that tasted good. And so, my search for a simple homemade wine-making method began.

I had a few criteria for the project: It had to be cheap, require very little in terms of equipment investment, and it had to consume relatively little time without cutting too far into my already busy days. The wine also had to include a minimum of ingredients – I wanted a natural product without having to invent a chemical signature; a product that did not require dumping a lot of unnecessary preservatives into the mix. More than anything, it had to be easy. Simple. A process my ten-year-old could follow (disclaimer: No minors were allowed to make or imbibe wine during the writing of this book).

After much research, I finally stumbled across the aforementioned Petersohn's site. His is an unassuming site without a lot of frills but with a healthy dose of character and good humor, and great back-to-basics wine-making information. Just the resource I needed. Petersohn's information, combined with some bits and pieces from a handful of other articles and sites, set the foundation for all of my in-home winemaking. Mr. Petersohn did in a few sentences what not a lot of others did – made me feel comfortable making good homemade wine "the old way" and kept it light, friendly and affordable. I've dabbled around with his basics for a number of years now, tweaked and experimented, strayed and enjoyed mostly successes but a few failures, too, and in the end stayed pretty close to his basics; I've passed this simple knowledge on to a number of interested homestead wine-making friends, grown tired of typing and repeating myself, and I'm now ready to share this most basic and manageable process to you for *your* enjoyment.

Mr. Petersohn, I understand from a very kind email exchange with his son, has, unfortunately, passed away; but his son has great memories of his father's passion for home wine making. He enjoys knowing that others share and benefit from this passion as well. I hope I do his process and memory credit. Although he is gone, to date his website remains to be found. You can find his web address in the references section.

Cheers to good, wholesome country knowledge! Let's make some wine!

HOW TO USE THIS BOOK

Perhaps it's obvious how you should use this book, but let me take a moment to guide you through it and present just a couple of options.

You could do the obvious: Read this book start-to-finish (which I do hope you'll do) and *then* set off on your home wine-making adventures. There's a lot to be gained by this traditional approach. You'll learn about the how's and the why's; you'll understand more about what makes wine happen, what makes wine *not* happen even though it should, and what makes wine vinegar. You'll learn the most basic things that wine needs in order to become drinkable and good, and you'll even learn a bit about the things I've left out – the more modern, more complex, more additive things; and why.

The first part of this book is all about the how's and why's and we talk a lot about very simple things like the equipment that you'll need, the cheap and easy options, how to make do with what you have and what you can buy downtown.

In the second part, we attack the process. We go through the process together step-by-step, and then summarize it into an actionable, basic, start-to-finish recipe before we move on to specific recipes, each with complete, easy-to-follow instructions. Along the way we'll also hit on how to change a recipe if ingredients or interests dictate.

There is, to be sure, a lot of information included here, but I've approached the process by tackling many of the questions I've come to ask myself over the ten or so years that I've been making simple (delicious, if I do say so) country wines.

If this feels overwhelming or too time-consuming, though, you could also pick around the parts and contents of this book to the pieces that you think you need to know in order to gain enough of an understanding, and then take off running. The Table of Contents should help you with that. In the interest of time, you might find it more suiting to skip ahead and try out a recipe or two and then reference back through the first part of the book when you find yourself not knowing a piece just yet.

Finally, know that there are several places where I have worked to give break-out, easy-use frameworks, tables, lists, and guidelines. These are available throughout the book in quick-reference style, and you will also find an addendum for faster, easier reference for things like shopping, buying and gathering equipment. At the risk of being redundant, you may come across remarkably similar resources in different parts of the book and in the resource section at the end. Maybe I repeat myself but I hope you find that as you come back to this book again and again for your latest and greatest wines, when you are more familiar with the process and the product, that these quick references and resources will be a valuable resource for you.

Please use this book in the way that it is most helpful to you. Use it to make winemaking easy and fun. Use it to experiment and to play. Read it, use it, and then use it again. And ENJOY how easy home winemaking can really be!

1

BUT FIRST, THE EQUIPMENT

"How the heck do you think your grandfather did it?"
(Frank Petersohn)

It seems two things keep people from making wine at home, and I'm not sure that one trumps the other. The investment in expensive wine-making equipment and what seems like a daunting, scientifically challenging and overwhelming process are the biggest reasons why people just say, "forget it." It's probably a toss-up to say which one of these issues we should tackle first, but it makes sense to start with the equipment list; this will give you the opportunity to start collecting and shopping while you learn the ropes, and also help ensure that you go into the process well set up, so you don't get caught short once you do get rolling.

It's very true that you can spend an awful lot on equipment to make homemade wine in an awfully short period of time. There's a lot of fancy stuff out there, with some very fancy price tags. But there is also some very cheap stuff available that really does do the job, and depending on your personal resources, you might find yourself able to get off really, really, cheap. With a little help from your friends, maybe even *free*.

BUCKETS FOR PRIMARY FERMENTATION

Let's start with your vessels for the primary fermentation. For this, what works best are large five gallon plastic buckets—like the kind you can buy in pretty much any hardware or big-box store. These typically cost only a few dollars apiece, with lids sold separately for another dollar or two. Don't worry about buying lids for now unless you think you might want them down the line. (Lids are optional because you don't need to tightly cover the bucket – more on that later.)

The batch size we like to work with is about a four- to five-gallon batch of finished product, which will give you quite a lot of homemade wine to enjoy throughout the year until next season. That said, some berries and fruits are not as abundant as others and you may or may not be inclined to pay for fruit and berries for your home wine making. This might be especially true in the beginning until you're convinced you'll have some success (although I have nothing but faith in you). Wine making is all about ratios, though, so it's not hard to cut a batch

Everyday 5-gallon pails from the local hardware store are easy, essential equipment.

down by percentages to suit the amount of fruit that you have available for a given batch. Thus, adjusting up or down from a recipe to use what's available to you is a simple matter.

Off on a tangent? Why all this talk about batch size now? To ensure that you have the right size buckets for your primary fermentation stage. Five-gallon plastic pails are best because they give you plenty of room for starting your wine and leaving enough headspace to keep the batch from bubbling over. you can always use a larger bucket that is larger than necessary at this stage, too, even if you are making a smaller batch because this is not a point where airspace is an issue. Still, just for the sake of manageability, if you can find a food-safe pail in something more towards a 2- or 3-gallon size, it's not a bad idea to pick it up and/or save it.

Now, we've thrown those phrases, "food-safe" or "food grade," around a little bit. Why are they important? Isn't a plastic bucket a plastic bucket? Kind of, but not really (and there's more specific information regarding identifying food-grade or food-safe plastic below). Basically, there are plastics that are manufactured and never intended to store or serve food or drink. The short of it is that your primary fermentation bucket will be something that your future libations will live in for at least a week, and something that you will be able to use over and over again; so taking an extra minute to make sure you are purchasing something food-safe is worth it. I've not found this to be much of a cost factor, it's more about accessibility and availability. What appears to be the case in recent years is that retailers perhaps just find it easier to offer a multi-use vessel. More and more I find that, without even trying, the five-gallon buckets in the hardware aisles usually *are* food-grade plastic anyway and are very frequently labelled as such.

Does it have to be new?

No, not really. That is, if you are sure about the history of your bucket and its former life. I wouldn't recommend grabbing up that old thing lying around in the garage, because you never know when someone has used it as a paint pail or to store or use toxic cleaning solutions and the like. Along with your bucket being food-grade, make sure that food is all that it has ever had in it. Other than that, wash it thoroughly and give it a sniff to see if you think there are any leftover tastes or odors that might color your wine. Usually a good airing-out and storing your buckets open so as not to trap in old flavors will do the trick.

Who do you know?

Got a baker friend? A deli owner pal? Maybe they just like you down at the local coffee shop?

Without realizing it, you may have a source of ideal food-grade buckets for making wine that may be free, or perhaps very, very cheap. Who do you know?

Do you have a friend who owns a local lunch shop? Know anyone working at a local bakery or bakery department in your local grocery store? Maybe just an approachable employee or manager? From pickles to pastry, batters and doughs, diners, restaurants, delis, bakeries, coffee shops, lunch counters...food-service establishments get all sorts of things in plastic buckets and pails that are just perfect after a little cleaning for using to make wine at home. They're already food-safe and they tend to become something of a nuisance for these establishments because they are bulky and pile up quickly from regularly used products. They can find only so many uses for them before they go into the trash or recycling, costing them good money to have them taken away. Often these places are happy to share, or sell for a pittance, if you just ask. It certainly doesn't hurt to try, and it will make your investment that much lower.

Food-safe by the numbers

Love it or leave it, but food-safe plastic will be your cheapest option for home wine making (and this applies to almost all of your wine-making equipment, not just your fermentation buckets). Now that we've touched upon the subject and you understand a little more about it, this is a good place to have a quick conversation about identifying food-safe and food-grade plastics before moving on to talk about the other equipment you'll need to gather.

Once you get looking around and sourcing cheap wine-making equipment, you'll find that food-grade plastic is not all that hard to find. I've found food-grade plastic vessels that are ideal for wine making at my local Wal Mart, hardware stores, even my local livestock and feed stores! And of course, you can find anything online. (Tip: When shopping, be sure to look in the actual hardware sections of these places; being larger and less popular items, that's often where you'll find them, not necessarily in a homewares or a grocery aisle.)

Pails will often be marked if they are food grade, but the numbers and symbols on the bottom indicate food safety as well.

The thing about plastic is that not all of it is considered food-safe (which is actually true of almost any type of material, including metals, glazed, and painted products, so no matter what you use, you really should be aware of its safety for making food-stuffs). There is a system in place to help us identify what is and isn't appropriate for food and drink.

The easiest way to identify food-safe buckets and bottles for making wine is to simply purchase vessels labelled as food safe or food grade. Yes, even five-gallon plastic buckets and lids sold in those feed stores and hardware aisles will often be labelled, loud and proud, as food safe.

Another way to help identify food grade plastics is to familiarize yourself with the grading system used for plastics classification. Plastics are graded on a number system ranging from one to seven. You will usually find this number on the bottom of the bottle or bucket, inside the triangle-shaped recycling arrow. These correspond with the type of plastic that the product is made from, as follows:

- #1: PET/PETE (typically used for grab-n-go bottled water and other drinks, not great for re-use)
- #2: *HDPE (most common food grade used for food grade buckets and water jugs, etc.)
- #4: LDPE
- #5: PP
- #3, #6, #7: *NOT FOOD SAFE*

Some #2 HDPE products are not always considered food grade. The reason for this is that sometimes buckets are manufactured using #2 plastic, but an additional release agent is used in the molding process that is not considered food grade. If you are looking for absolute safety, look for some additional qualification along with the number. For example, a label stating the bucket is food safe or food grade, an additional cup and fork symbol near the number, a logo or symbol of an authoritative body such as USDA, FDA, or NSF—any of these will indicate an approved, food-grade product.

Shopping List

What you need:

- Minimum of 1, 5-gallon food-grade plastic bucket, lid optional (2 buckets are recommended for easier straining and transferring)

Additional to consider:

- 2-3 (or more) buckets if you plan to do a lot of wine making, or might have more than one batch going at the same time (remember, each batch will stay in this primary fermenter for about a week)
- One or more smaller, 2-3-gallon buckets for smaller batches of more limited fruits

CHEESECLOTH OR PLASTIC WRAP TO KEEP THE BUGS AT BAY

While not strictly necessary, it's not a bad idea to have something on hand to cover the bucket during your first fermentation. To be clear: DO NOT COVER THE VESSEL TIGHTLY; i.e., do not secure the bucket cover. As fermentation progresses, carbon dioxide gas is produced. It acts as something of a natural protectant, but it will also build up pressure. If you put a tight cover on the bucket, you are likely to blow it off after a few days.

At this point, all you are really going for is something to help manage fruit flies and falling objects (fruit flies can't really live in the wine and environment so even if a few are around, don't worry). A doubled layer of cheesecloth is helpful and lets gasses escape. It's not usually my first choice because sometimes the weave can be

Cheap linen towels make good covers for primary fermentation and come in handy many times along the wine making way.

quite large or uneven and can still let those mysterious little fliers in; so, you do want to at least double it. An elastic band around the outside edge of the bucket is helpful to keep the cloth in place. Cheesecloth can also be a little pricey, but it does have the benefit of being reusable. A covering of plastic wrap works well, too; poke holes with a pin in several places to let gasses escape but keep bugs out. My simplest and easiest solution is a large, linen towel (sometimes called "flour sack" towels). You'll find out quickly that with wine, it's a lot about what you let out, without letting things in.

Shopping List

What you need:

- 1 package of cheesecloth per batch or
- Plastic wrap or
- Large linen "flour sack" towels

Additional to consider:

- Large rubber bands, large enough to stretch around the outer perimeter of the bucket (for large buckets, elastic trash barrel bands work well)
- Kitchen thermometer to measure temperature of the must (the crushed fruit) before pitching (adding) the yeast

LARGE JUGS OR CARBOYS FOR SECONDARY FERMENTATION AND RACKING

The second stage of the process will require something more protected. For cheap and easy homemade wine, my vessel of choice for secondary fermentation and racking is a simple large water cooler jug. Again, you'll find me using plastic.

Traditional supply houses will recommend what is called a "carboy" or "demijohn"; it's really just a different version of a water cooler jug, traditionally made of glass but suppliers are offering more plastic versions now, too. The thing about glass is that in addition to being expensive to begin with, it is also very heavy even before you add five gallons of liquid to it. Heft makes shipping expensive if you are buying online, and makes full jugs of wine heavy to handle. Trust me when I say that even the plastic jugs can be heavy and awkward to handle when filled (and this is something to consider if lifting or back issues are part of your life…it might be best for you to consider a couple of smaller jugs rather than one large one for this stage).

There are a few things that make plastic water cooler jugs my choice for secondary fermentation. First among them is our requirement that things be as cheap as possible, and these are the cheapest things I've found for this function. As mentioned, these jugs are lightweight and are the most easily handled out of the available options. They're already food safe. And they're really very easy to find pretty much anywhere you live. I find some excellent cheap options from retailers like Wal Mart and Amazon online. Even though they are big, they are so lightweight they ship cheaply and it's easy to find retailers like Wal Mart or Amazon that will ship for free for a low price threshold purchase. Consolidate your shopping list with one or two sellers, spend $30 or so and you're probably in business with your equipment list done. Even shopping locally, though, these jugs aren't hard to find, even if you have to buy the water and dump it. Once again…who do you know? Anyone with an old water cooler jug or two kicking around??

These water jugs are available starting around 6-7$ and in a variety of sizes. A variety of sizes, while not strictly necessary, is nice because you won't always have enough of a quantity of certain fruits or berries to make a large five-gallon batch. As we'll talk about a little later, the real enemy to making good wine as opposed to good vinegar is keeping air out of the product. And so, the less space you have left in your vessel for air to be in, the more likely your success and the better your wine will be. You can typically source cheap, BPA-free, food-grade water bottles from big-box stores and online retailers for much less than you can purchase carboys from brew supply houses. Those glass carboys usually start around 30$ before shipping (and shipping on heavy glass products can be steep). To compare, I recently ordered a one-gallon jug, two three-gallon, a five-gallon, and replacement caps on walmart.com all for the same $30 (with that free shipping).

Water cooler-type plastic jugs come in a variety of sizes and make ideal cheap "carboys" for home wine making.

Though my recommendation is plastic I'm certainly not opposed to those nice glass carboys and vessels, except for the price and the heft of them. Plastic is pretty easy to source at your local store and can get you into winemaking without too much outlay, but certainly feel free to indulge and invest if you prefer, or upgrade as you get your wine-making legs and a little confidence in your practice behind you!

Shopping List

What you need:

- 1 large, 5-gallon plastic water jug per batch (reusable, but each batch will keep the jug in use for at least 1 month)

Additional to consider:

- Additional 5-gallon plastic water jugs for other batches
- Plastic water jugs in various sizes for smaller batches; 1-gallon and 3-gallon jugs in addition to the 5-gallon make for a nice, rounded equipment stock
- Replacement caps for wine storage and racking (optional)

TUBING OR AIRLOCKS AND A GLASS JAR OR TWO

The key to making wine and not vinegar is to control the contact that the fermenting brew has with air. To an extent, the process does this naturally, because fermentation produces carbon dioxide gas, which is heavier than air so as it is produced, it creates a sort of gaseous blanket over the top of the surface of the wine-to-be. If you could be sure that your vessel will never get bumped or moved, that it will produce that protective blanket quickly enough to prevent air contamination and to keep bugs and other nasties out, then in theory you could go without an airlock of some sort. Really, though, an airlock is important once you move to the second fermentation step. And no, the cover to your bucket or water jug will not do. Why not? Because that gas will soon result in a buildup of pressure, too...and completely sealed vessels that don't let the air and excess gas escape out of the way as the gas is produced soon become household bombs. So tight lids and sealed covers are not for use at this stage.

What you need to achieve is a system in which air and excess gas can be pushed out of the vessel without allowing air back in. In modern wine-making with modern supplies, airlocks are sold. It's very important, though, that you make sure your airlock is either exactly the size of your jug cap or that it can be fitted to it without leaving any opportunity for

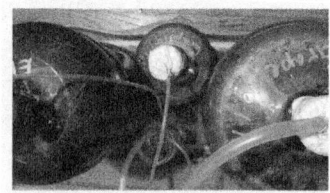

Airlocks can be made with a few easily-obtained items, all of which you can find in local stores.

air to infiltrate your fermenter. Some have come down in price and so may be worth looking at, but for our cheap-and-easy-no-frills-no-big-investment wine-making process, we can do an excellent job with just a few supplies from the local shop (or maybe your junk drawer).

All you will need is the cover that your water jug already came with, some sturdy scissors or razor knife, a roll of duct tape, a glass jar, and a length of tubing (aquarium tubing is perfect and really easy to find locally for a dollar or two). It doesn't have to be food safe, but it can be if you prefer (your tubing may just be rated food safe anyway, so give it a look). For this use the tubing won't come into contact with the wine so food-grade is optional; however, later in the process you'll need tubing for siphoning, so it's not a bad idea to locate something food grade and buy a good-sized roll that will cover all your needs...four to six feet will give you plenty for everything. For small money, food-safe tubing is readily available online. The diameter of the tubing for the airlock isn't important; for siphoning a larger size (½ inch) gives more volume to make things move faster but as an airlock piece any small tube is fine...it's only a gaseous escape route.

There is one other very cheap airlock option that some people like, and the only items necessary are a balloon and pin to poke holes in the balloon. Some people do experience some difficulty with balloons popping off or ripping or breaking, but it's definitely a cheap option that works when it works and might be worth your time to try.

Shopping List

What you need:

- Length of tubing (18-24 inches will suffice for the airlock)
- Bottle cap or cover (typically comes with the bottle)
- Duct tape
- Glass jar

Additional to consider:

- Balloon if you wish to try the balloon airlock method
- Pin for poking holes
- 4 to 6 feet of food-safe tubing to be used for both creating an airlock and for cutting a length for siphoning
- Brewing or fermenting airlocks (but you must be sure they can be fitted specifically to your vessel)

SOMETHING TO MASH YOU WITH, MY DEAR

Fruits and berries need to be crushed and mushed in order to release their juices to turn into wine. If somehow you (or a very kind friend) have a fruit crusher and/or cider or wine press, you'll be one happy winemaker indeed. Use that. Most of us starting out don't happen to have this equipment, though, and that equipment doesn't come cheap. No worries; there are plenty of cheap and free options to serve this purpose. In fact, this is about the cheapest piece of equipment you'll need.

Different fruits and berries have varying levels of crushability, so what you choose to use for one might be a little different for the next. All you really need to do the job is a sturdy hand masher (potato or fruit masher, for example). Actually, I find that for many fruits, and especially for berries, what works best is your own two hands. Very simply, just get your hands in there and start crushing and squeezing. Take out your aggressions. Relieve some stress. It's not pretty. It's not complicated. It's just plain destroying fruit. All you will really need to do is work through the bowl or bucket and crush open as many of the fruits or berries as possible, mangling them to release as much juice as possible. No, you won't get every drop out but that's okay, because that leftover mass of mush is what will become your "must" and it will continue to break down and release juice and flavor as the fruit ferments—you're just making sure that you can get it a nice, juicy, flavorful head start.

While not absolutely necessary, what I do suggest is that you buy a box of cheap latex or vinyl gloves or buy a pair or two of rubber kitchen gloves. For one thing, berries and fruits can stain your skin and nails, which isn't a big deal, but sometimes you get tired of explaining away your sudden dark purpleness and having to repeatedly quell fears that you are perhaps having some oxygen deprivation issue. Fruits and berries can also have irritants under the skins (I find wild grapes and elderberries to be particular offenders); and then some of us just have easily irritated skin to begin with, so a pair of gloves is a cheap and easy skin-saver that can save you some scratching later on.

A kitchen blender or food processor is yet another tool that can help to crush the fruits and berries for juicing and wine making. You only want to use this, though, if you are working with fruit with an easily removable seed. Berries and small fruits do not usually qualify, and neither will wild or seeded grapes. The seeds of fruits and berries often contain elements that can be poisonous and/or irritating on some level. If they are intact it's not a problem but if you use something like a food processor with blades that will nick and open the seeds, you risk releasing that into your wine. It's a potential health and safety issue and it has the potential to become a flavor issue as well. So, unless you are going to pit or seed the ingredients first, do not run them through anything that will break the seeds. Obviously, you can't de-seed tiny little berries like raspberries, blackberries, or elderberries, et cetera, and so blending and processing is not a great option for berries, but as easy as they are to mash by hand, it's almost not worth the trouble of machine processing anyway.

Shopping List:

Consider purchasing:

- Latex, vinyl, or rubber gloves
- Kitchen food masher

STRAINING CLOTHS OR DEVICES

After that crushed must has made its most fabulous of transformations, it'll need to be strained and separated from the young liquid wine. This will happen after about a week of primary fermentation.

Many things work well for this purpose. It's worth a good look around your kitchen and supplies to see if you might already have something that will do the trick. What you're looking for is something with a very fine straining capability that will collect the big pieces and most of the fines. Don't feel that you need something that will catch all of the very fine particles; you'll nearly always have a little of that coming through at this point and that is okay; as the wine goes through its next stages those fine particles and many other things will "fall out" and settle in the bottom of your fermenter. It's a normal stage of the wine-making process, no matter how fancy, invested, and involved you get. We'll deal with how to separate your finished wine from that later but for now, know that what you are striving for is to get the pieces of the fruit or berries, any random stems and seeds and any sizable pieces of "must" out of the wine to get it ready for that second fermentation.

Some things that I have used that work well include regular kitchen strainers and fine-mesh strainers. I often work these in a variety of sizes because all strainers will plug up a little and I find that if I run the biggest of the chunks out through a large-holed colander or strainer first, it gets rid of the bulk of it quickly and easily and I can then work down to my finest sieves to keep removing smaller refuse.

Jelly bags and strainers, like what hangs on a metal frame to strain fruit for jelly-making, have worked well, as have clean linen kitchen towels (cheap ones like flour sack towels that you won't mind staining and probably relegating to this kind of use). A cheesecloth-lined colander isn't a bad way to go, but because the weave in cheesecloth is so open, stretchable, and varied, it usually takes a few layers of it and cheesecloth can be rather pricey so it's not my first choice. What Frank Petersohn liked to recommend was buying up a stock of new, cheap nylon pantyhose, and cutting out the legs. Buy the biggest size you can find, and you can even stretch them over the mouth of a five-gallon bucket. If you have a spot to tie it off and hang it for a little while over your bucket, you'll collect a lot of the trapped wine, too, and salvage just that much more good juice.

Because we also keep bees, some of our honey-straining equipment serves good double-duty here. Honey is often extracted into buckets as well and beekeeping equipment suppliers make fine strainers in graduated mesh sizes that fit right over the top of a five-gallon bucket. It's more expense, but they work well and are readily available online.

Finally, wine-making suppliers sell mesh fermenting or pulp bags that you can use for straining. Alternatively, you can use the same bags in the fermenting juice to contain the pulp. When it is time to remove the pulp from the juice, instead of straining the must, you simply lift the bag of pulp out of the juice. Most are reusable many times, but they do have some cost to them. You can find similar bags that will do the trick for sale with fruit- and cider-pressing equipment, and they may be cheaper than those from wine suppliers. If you're handy with a sewing machine, you could probably make them cheaply from linen kitchen towels. Old-time jelly-makers and cider-makers have been known to use cheap pillowcases for similar jobs, and those would work well, too!

Shopping List:

One or a combination of the following options:

- Colander
- Linen towels or cheesecloth
- Jelly strainer with straining bag
- New clean nylon hose, extra-large size
- Fine mesh strainer(s) (one will do the job but it's helpful and faster to have a couple on hand)

Additional to consider:

- Straining equipment made for other homesteading tasks, such as straining honey or maple syrup, or perhaps a kitchen cone strainer
- Fermentation bag or fruit-pressing bag

DUCT TAPE

Duct tape? Really? Yes, duct tape. Insert jokes at will, but duct tape is a cheap and easy fix that will help you easily fit your cheap and easy wine-making supplies and will also be a handy go-to for sealing up caps and lids and who knows what else to keep the air out. In a pinch, it can even *be* a cap. Trust me. grab a roll or two. have it on hand. It doesn't even have to be the expensive stuff.

Shopping List:

What you need:

- 1 roll of inexpensive duct tape

BOTTLES FOR LONG-TERM STORAGE

Between one and three months into the process, after your first and second fermentations are complete, it will be time to store your wine for the long term and/or to let it age until it's ready to use. You might decide at this point to "rack" it for a bulk storage and some more aging (more on that later), but regardless, there will come a time when you need to bottle your wine into manageable, go-to portions that will allow you to serve your wine without exposing the unused portions and ruining the rest of the batch. You'll need to bottle your wine.

What you're basically looking for is containers that can be filled with little headspace leftover (so nothing too large) and that can be firmly sealed. Wine bottles, of course, are ideal. While new wine bottles are readily available through wine and brew supplies and online, there's nothing wrong with saving yourself some money and reusing old wine bottles that are free from cracks and chips. Cork or screw-top doesn't matter (but if you are reusing screw tops make sure the top still functions well and is sealable or can be replaced with a cork). So, start collecting. ask your friends to save their wine bottles. Collect a variety of sizes and mix it up when you bottle — that way you can choose the right serving size for a crowd, or a smaller bottle for just yourself or you and your plus one, and you won't be stuck with too much left over to turn to vinegar.

Keep in mind that if you are reusing bottles, whether collected and recycled or reused from your last batches, the *corks* from those bottles should not be reused. You'll have compromised the corks from opening them with the corkscrew, they'll have expanded, and they'll start falling apart. Don't let your good wine go to waste by being too cheap with old corks!

Of course, in order to tightly cork your bottles, you'll need a way to set the corks. This is not something you can do by hand and trust it to keep your wine air-free and well-preserved. This requires a corker. These are available in a range of prices, but a decent corker for home winemaking can be had in the twenty- to thirty-dollar range. With it, you'll need to buy fresh corks. These are pretty cheap, too, and available in different numbered sizes. A bag of number 8 or number 9 corks will fit most any bottles you might collect. Note: "Mushroom" style corks *can* be pushed in by hand and do not require a corker, if you're up to it (they do require some brute strength). There are also styles like the push-in plastic-topped corks that don't require additional equipment. If you think you might use one of these types, it's not a bad idea to order them ahead of time and try out how hard they are to use; you don't want to find out that you can't get your cork in with 20 bottles of wine laid out ahead of you.

Is this starting to sound pricy? Are we still talking about *cheap* and easy winemaking here?

A little more investment in the final storage vessels is necessary so that all that hard work doesn't wind up being labor-intensive salad dressing. There are other options, varying in price and outlay but also in reusability, to help you get around the initial expense. The following ideas will give you some options for starting cheap and small and then building up and investing later on as you get your wine-making legs under you.

Mr. Petersohn suggests saving and reusing two-liter soda bottles and caps. It's not an option I've personally tried but others have and it's certainly a cheap way to go (if you are a soda drinker). As mentioned before, reusing saved wine bottles or other similar glass bottles that either have good screw caps or can be corked is a very good way to go. Start collecting and ask your friends. A little rinsing and boiling water make for easy cleaning and sterilization.

Many types, sizes, and styles of bottles can be used for bottling wine.

Mason jars and canning jars are also a fair option. The greatest benefit to these is that they come with caps and lids, which are perfectly capable of giving you the tight seal you need to maintain your wine's quality without having to invest in more equipment likes corks and corkers. What's more, the caps and lids (because you are not actually canning and heat treating) are reusable for as long as they are in decent, rust-free shape; and even when they begin to show a bit too much use, they're cheap and easy to replace. Canning jars also have the benefit of being available in a variety of sizes, including up to half-gallon size, for bottling in varying amounts. If you're feeling on the fence about using either reused soda bottles or mason jars for reasons of presentation, just remember you can always grab a nice glass decanter or two for serving, or do a mix-and-match of nicer storage vessels and utilitarian ones like the jars for when presentation is a little less of a concern. The risk you run with mason jars is a wider mouth and hence a little bit more surface air exposure, but I've stored in them before and they're not a bad way to go. If tightly sealed with little headspace, they do the job.

Swing-top bottles can be found online and often in home goods sections of your local store or where canning supplies are sold. These make nice one-step bottling and capping options that look very nice as well, are reusable, and present very well if gift-giving or serving at a nice meal. The price range can be all over the place, though, so they aren't always the best cheap option, but long-term they do last, require no additional equipment outlay for corks and corking, and so might be something you want to consider.

Shopping List:

What you'll need:

- Wine bottles
- Screw caps or fresh corks or
- Other alternative storage vessels and caps listed below

Additional to consider:

- Corker for corking bottles (needed if storing and capping with corks)
- Mason or canning jars with two-piece lids in good condition
- Swing-top bottles
- Soda bottles with caps
- Other recyclable bottles, jars, or containers, glass preferred, with tight-fitting lids in good condition
- One or two wine decanters or pitchers for serving

FEELING CONFUSED?

If, at this point, you find yourself feeling a little bit confused as to what you will be doing with all these odds and ends of equipment, don't fear. Some of these pieces may make obvious sense; others might seem a little boggling in regard to how you will use them. Soon, though, we'll move on and walk through the actual wine-making process step by step. As we do, we'll lay out exactly how to use the supplies on our list, right down to how to create that crazy airlock with a piece of tubing and some duct tape. For now, just start looking around and compiling. I urge you to read through the book to get a grasp of how the process of winemaking goes from start to finish, and then things will start to become clearer. For where we are now, it's enough to just start learning about the tools and supplies you will need to give you a jump start on collecting and compiling and feeling out your more personal and local resources so that you're ready when it does come time to make that first batch of wine.

2

SOURCING YOUR FRUITS

There are so very, very many fruits (and even vegetables) that can be used for making homemade wine. So, where do you find them?

Where your fruit comes from will depend a lot on your particular situation and what is readily available to you. Many people come to home wine making because they enjoy some level of gardening, amateur orcharding, or grape- or berry-growing. Our own personal venture into home wine making was based a lot on similar circumstances - we were already milking a backyard dairy animal or two for milk for the home, growing a large garden in two plots for a combined total of about half an acre in berries and vegetables, and then we discovered, during our first fall on our new property, that we were truly blessed with an abundance of wild New England grapes climbing all over the stone walls and trees on our property. As the kids went back to school, the scent of ripe wild grapes, a true mark of early fall in New England, just beckoned us to do something with them. My sister turns hers into gallons of juice which she freezes for later year-long enjoyment along with batches of great homemade jelly. I enjoy a good couple of batches of grape jelly as well, but the bulk of our harvest goes first into good, old-fashioned homemade wine.

Whether you are as blessed as we are with nature's gifts, or whether you live in an apartment in the city with nary a wild grape or berry around, you can still source great things to make great homemade wine. We'll take a look here at some very good options.

FORAGING FOR FLAVOR

What's in your own backyard?

Your own backyard is the very best place to start. And you shouldn't wait until fall happens to think about what excellent natural resources you might have that might make great wine. We start our wine-making year months ahead of autumn. It usually starts with the earliest berries. And those berries make some truly delicious, flavorful wines; among our best, in fact.

The first fruits of the season are almost always berries — strawberries first, followed by raspberries and blueberries in quick succession, then into blackberries, and our hands-down favorite homemade wine base, the elderberry. All of these are native berries that grow wild in our local area, and so with a little effort, kind words with friends and neighbors (greased perhaps with the promise of a bit of homemade), and some time spent foraging and picking, I can easily find delicious berries right here in my own backyard, completely for free.

Foraged berries are probably one of the easiest wine-making ingredients to come by. Of them, blackberries are a personal favorite—once you locate a good stand or two of blackberries, you'll figure out that they spread easily if left unchecked and unchoked. They're a pioneering species so look toward places that have been cleared and let go in recent years. They are large as wild berries go, prolific, and easily give you a wine with excellent flavor.

If there is a downside to making wine with foraged berries, it is that they can be harder to find in quantity for larger batches. Usually any wines I make with foraged berries tend to be smaller batches because they just don't add up in weight or volume the way large fruits and things like grapes do. Generally, I wait and see what the crop is going to be, and then I just plan for the most appropriate size batch; to give you an idea, batches for berry wines usually trend more towards the one- to three- gallon range.

Even before the berries come ready, and/or often alongside them, there are blooms and blossoms that can be used for making wine, varying by where you live. Dandelions proliferate almost anywhere and are one of the first of the edible blossoms for both bees and winemakers alike. In "these parts" here in New England, the elderberry blossoms pop in late June and into the first part of July, and these are known to make excellent teas, liqueurs, and yes, excellent wine.

We also happen to be quite blessed on our property and our local area with a couple of varieties of wild grapes. Again, they are what inspired us to go into home winemaking, and what pushed me to follow my instinct and find a simple way to do it. About the time the kids go back to school, you start smelling these grapes along the roadsides and on the edges of yards and wooded areas if they've been allowed to take hold. They add up fast and they are, of course, the most obvious of our natural ingredients.

Most likely you have some idea of the local edible fruits and berries that grow around you. If you do not personally have wild fruits and berries growing on your property, someone near you likely does so take the time to look around your property, and the properties of friendly neighbors, family, and abutters. Take some mental inventory. See what is growing freely for your use. Chat with the friendly locals in the know, most especially the older crowd. Do a little research (and you'll get plenty of ideas here in later chapters, too). More often than not, you'll find that most ingredients that are picked and used for juices, jellies, and jams are also good wine-making candidates. From chokecherries to crabapples, quite often cheap, quality ingredients are closer at hand than you'll know.

WHAT CAN YOU GROW?

If you do a bit of gardening or growing, look towards what you already have established, what you can establish in relatively short time, and what you can plant now with an eye to the future.

Even some of the less obvious crops can be used in wine making. It's said that rhubarb makes a nice, light wine (with varying results reported in terms of acidity and harshness, much owing to age) and can also be used with other fruits and berries like strawberries or cherries. Pumpkin wine is supposed to taste towards a chardonnay. Beet wine is said to have a certain earthiness and an absolutely gorgeous color. Tomato wine reportedly is slightly sweet and spicy, and better than you'd ever imagine.

While I can't say that I've personally made wine with each and every one of these ingredients, the point is that many, many fruits and vegetables, too, have been used for years and years to make what are now considered "country wines" (country wines being, essentially, what we are talking about in this book — wines made with the fruits of the earth that are available, cheaply, in the old way...as simply and effectively as possible). And while certain crops like rhubarb take a year or two to establish, others like beets, tomatoes, and pumpkins are seasonal growers that can give you some interesting ingredients to play with in a relatively short period of time.

Now, or perhaps after a successful batch or two, might be the time to look toward the future and what potential wine-making ingredients you might want to start. Most of the more mainstream crops used for winemaking take a year to a few years to establish to the point of real usefulness. Strawberries and rhubarb planted this year should give you a good next-season yield (although rhubarb, depending on the age of the crowns and/or whether you plant from bare root or started potted plants may take up to two). More bush-type berries often take two to three years to be productive. Of course, grapes are an obvious wine crop to think toward; these, too, generally take three years to harvest.

In addition to grapes, vegetables, and berries, orchard fruits are great wine-making candidates. Apples, plums, cherries, peaches, pears, and more are all fairly easily grown over time, with just a tree or two providing plenty for your winemaking pleasure and many other canning, baking, preserving, and fresh uses, too. Of course, these require a bit more of a long-term investment in your property, but relative to your circumstances, they're most definitely worth considering. Sure, it may seem now that such long-term crop investments for your wines are just too far off from yielding, but as we all come to learn too soon, time passes quickly and those things you plant today can be reliable, quality, trustworthy sources of fruit and berries for many, many years to come, with enough versatility for not just home wine-making, but so much more.

VINEYARDS, ORCHARDS AND PICK YOUR OWN

Clearly not all of us have the time, money, or land resources to plant long-term home wine-making crops. Even those of us who do often find that we need to set ourselves some limits. Regardless of your personal situation, you can still make excellent country wines without ever growing a thing. Some of our thumbs are just more red or white than green.

For those crops that I either do not personally grow or forage or cannot grow or forage in enough abundance to make a sizable batch of wine, I frequently turn to the next best thing: Local pick your own, or PYO.

Pick your own crops are a win-win in my book. You get to load up in a pretty short amount of time on the freshest local ingredients for your home wine making. You have the opportunity to do a little local research and find the growers who are raising their crops in line with your own personal goals and beliefs, whether those goals relate to crop freshness, organic production, crop type, growing processes, or another goal or belief that is important to you. When you buy locally at the source of production you usually have the option of connecting with someone very much in the know about a given farm's management and practices, and you can learn a lot about not only *how* the crops are grown but a lot about the varieties on offer. Growers are very knowledgeable about the specific types of fruit and vegetables that they have chosen to grow and can often guide you to something special and most well-suited to your wine-making goals. What's more, when you buy at the source you might even find that you have a wider variety of varieties, such as heirlooms and lesser-known types not typically available in more commercial streams. This is often because some of the most flavorful and nutrient-dense fruits and vegetables do not ship well or do not store well for months on end. As a result, the commercial markets have turned to varieties that in the end offer us a great ability to take a beating and endure long weeks and months in shipment and in storage, but at a loss to higher standards of taste and nutrition.

PYO is a win for you because it allows you to buy in bulk at the source in a well-tended, well-planned environment optimized for fast, easy picking; and since you are basically providing your own harvest labor, it'll be at a reduced price compared to retail. Farmers and growers win because you are supporting their business and helping to reduce their labor costs. They avoid losing money to a third-party middleman seller and are making more sales, which in turn helps to keep their farm going (which means continued good local resources, open space, fresh air, and all of those other great things that go along with local agriculture...I may be a bit of a fan).

The most obvious examples of PYO are orchards that offer apple picking. These are often a source of other orchard fruits like peaches, plums, pears, apricots, cherries and more. One thing to keep in mind is that many of these crops are staggered throughout the growing season and will be ready and available much earlier, and for a more limited time, than apples, so it's worth a little research well ahead of time to find out what might be growing and picking, and when. Other popular PYO crops to think about for making wine include many of the berries we talked about before – strawberries, blueberries, raspberries, and blackberries are all available PYO options.

Fruits and berries tend to be the most obvious and best-advertised local wine-making options for direct-source buying, but you might be surprised to learn that buying grapes for winemaking at a not-too-distant vineyard or grower might be an option, too. The availability of locally-sourced grapes is definitely a more limited crop, but they are out there, and a little internet searching might just turn up more resources than you'd expect. Like everything, grapes have their season so when buying direct in this way you'll need to be aware of the general time for ripening and availability; so once again, forethought never hurts.

One final thing to think about at orchards and PYO farms is whether they offer reduced-price "seconds" or "drops." These are fruits that may have fallen off the tree or bush due to ripening or weather, but which are still in perfectly usable condition, save for a few bruises, scarred or marred skins, or they might be a bit small in size for retail sale. (A bit of bruising on fruit in your wine is not a big deal. As long as it's not extensive, and the fruit is not actually spoiling, you'll only need to cut away bad spots back to good flesh.) Most often there's really nothing wrong with the fruit at all, except that it might be a little "ugly", and retail buyers just don't like ugly fruit; but seconds are perfect for things like sauces, jellies, and *wine*. Orchards and farms will often prefer to sell these "seconds" at a reduced price and typically in a larger bulk unit. In fact, I can often buy these "less desirable" fruits at the source and they look far better than what is on offer at the local grocery after it's been stored, shipped, and bumped around. Seconds are my go-to resource for most of what I do in my own kitchen and for wine ingredients that I'm not growing or foraging myself.

GROWERS, FARM STANDS, AND FARMERS' MARKET FAVORITES

Your local farm stands, roadside stands, and farmers' markets are other top places to look for wine-making produce. Again, your options will be tied to the growing season, so a regular visit, a conversation, and some forethought are all good ideas so that you don't miss your favorites. Farmers' markets and farm stands lend many of the same benefits of PYO, and you don't have to do the picking (but the price may reflect that convenience). Like PYO, on-site farm purchases and buying at farmers' markets give you the opportunity to talk directly with growers and employees who can help you with your decisions and offer opportunities to learn about how your fruit grows.

Buying at farmers' markets and on-site at farms and farm stands should give you more bulk-buying options, but it also behooves you to talk with your farmer (always such a great idea anyway) ahead of time to plan larger bulk purchases. This courtesy helps you to plan ahead and know when what you are looking for might become available but also helps the farmer to know to bring enough of a supply or have enough harvested and ready for pickup for you.

It's also worth having a polite and respectful conversation over price. Often farmers and growers are happy to give a good customer a bit of a discount when buying in large quantity, and growers will always prefer making a sale – especially a known sale – rather than seeing great fruits and vegetables go to waste. Let them know that your intention is to make wine and that something a little bruised or "seconds" are perfectly acceptable to you, and they'll be even more likely to work with you on price. Often growers will offer up great deals on various crops when they have a bumper crop, especially for crops they consider to be canning or processing quality. Following your grower on social media for overstocks, deals, and sales or otherwise staying in communication with them can often result in some good buys for wine-making crops and more.

THE WORLD OF FRUIT ONLINE

I'm not sure we should be surprised that nearly anything can be purchased online, but grapes for making wine were probably one of the farthest things down my list. Yet it's true. Even fresh grapes for making wine can be purchased online and shipped directly to you. In addition, you can purchase various dehydrated fruits and berries which can be boiled, reconstituted, and steeped to make a juice base for wine (not the most ideal process and more suited to some, such as elderberries, than others). Ready-to-go grape wine musts are available online, too.

Online buying options, however, will only get a quick mention here, and the reason for that is that buying fruits online doesn't exactly meet our criteria for cheap (although, depending, "easy" probably fits the bill pretty well). Shipping for these items can be quite high on top of the cost of the product itself. So yes, worth a mention, but no, probably not where you want to start trialing your wine making. This might be an option to keep in mind for the future once you have some experience under your belt, and if you're really looking for a specific wine grape (like a traditional chardonnay, for example), it's one way to access those hard-to-find ingredients.

VINTNER'S JUICES, CONCENTRATES, AND OTHER JUICES

If you do need to turn to an alternate source fruit base, a better option over buying fresh fruit or musts is buying the fruit already in juice form. If you do some searching online for things like "make wine from juice", or "make wine from juice concentrate," you'll see that there definitely are people out there doing it, even just from regular grape juice made for drinking fresh. It might be worth some playing, but you're not talking a real country wine here, and you have to look quite a lot into the contents of a specific juice brand and be very aware of the effects that preservatives and other additives might have on your wine. Even if you are a good label reader, it can be tough to decipher what is really fruit juice, concentrated juice, what percentage of concentration the juice is, and so on (a lot of this owing to vague and permissive labelling laws). At the end of the day it seems that for the outlay and outcome, you're not really getting much toward the goal of cheap, easy, and authentic. Even still, we're all about easing the "rules" of home wine making and making it more enjoyable, so if it strikes you as worth a try, please do. Just do a little looking into it first.

A much better option to grocery store juices and juice concentrates is to purchase juice sold specifically for making wine, often called vintner's juice, wine base, or fruit base. Vintner's juices are fairly readily available online and at homebrew and home wine-making supply stores (if you are lucky enough to have a good local resource). People do seem to have mixed results with vintner's juices, too, so it may take some playing to get just the results you are looking for; but then again, wine making is pretty much just that, anyway—a lot to do with personal taste and expectations, and a fair amount of playing around to get it there. Like Mr. Petersohn, my personal approach is to not go into it with too much of an expectation that your wine will come out like a commercial Merlot or Pinot, but instead go into it with the premise that good, simple, country wine has a lot to offer too, and if you can do it cheaply and simply enough with some healthy curiosity, you can have a lot of fun developing your own personal country wines that will be quite unique and specific to you (and yes, delicious!).

If you do turn to vintner's juices or wine bases, there are some things you can consider doing to enhance the flavor of the juice and the resulting wine. One of the biggest complaints against vintner's juice concentrates is that the resulting wines are thin or weaker in flavor than desired and that sometimes the wines lose flavor over time. Some of these juices can come off as having a "cooked" flavor as well, owing to the extraction, processing, and packing process. Here are a few things you can try to make a more full-bodied wine with wine bases:

- **Start with the lower concentration instructions.** A lot of these juices include different batch sizes (three or five gallons, for example).
- **Back-flavor with more concentrate.** "Back-flavor" simply means to add more flavor, such as when you add additional unfermented juice or concentrate. (Either reserve a portion at the beginning and freeze it until the wine is finished and ready for back-flavoring, or buy more concentrate and add it back into the wine at the end).
- **Back-flavor with another wine or another complementary flavor.** Choose something complementary to the wine you are making. If using wine (maybe one of your own, maybe a purchased bottle), generally speaking, use reds for darker fruits, whites or blushes for lighter berries, or simply whatever strikes your fancy as interesting enough to try. People also use things like extracts or other types of complementary juices and fruit nectars.

- **Back-sweeten.** Back-sweetening simply means to add more sugar syrup, such as simple syrup (which is just sugar dissolved in water, usually in equal parts). To fruits, sugar is a support to their flavor, the level of sweetness of a fruit or berry being a top factor in how we perceive its taste, and a reason that we have "good" and "bad" grape, berry, or fruit years. The reason to add additional sugar in at the end is so that the fermentation process (sugar conversion process by the yeast) has completed and therefore the sweetness will stay as a flavor and not be more fuel for the fire (which has the potential of creating some truly fiery wine!). This is usually done right before bottling. More by-the-book winemakers will instruct you to also add a stabilizing agent when you back-sweeten, Campden tablets or potassium sorbate in particular, to kill off any remaining yeasts and prevent restarting fermentation. These are, essentially, adding either preservatives or additional sulfites (common preservatives in food and wine). This means you will be adding preservative to your product, and is a decision you need to make for yourself depending on your "wine goals").

(*For my money, back-flavoring and back-sweetening options are pretty good ways to start off, especially if you are new to winemaking, because it gives you the opportunity to just try it out the simplest way possible, with the juice, and then play and doctor things up at the end if you're not happy with the initial outcome. You can always experiment with small samples of the batch without risking the whole thing, but who knows? You might find you don't need to fool with it at all! Often, that will be the case.)*

- **Adding additional ingredients to the fruit base**. You'd do this much as you would use complementary ingredients to make wine from a must and then leaving the ingredients in the juice throughout the primary fermentation process. There are different ways to go about this. For example, the addition of raisins or citrus/citrus peel can help support flavor and fill out a base like elderberry juice. Many recipes for elderberry wine, even when made from fresh berries, include ingredients such as these. A good way to go about it is to look up some recipes and get ideas about additional complementary flavors.

- **Adding real crushed fruit.** If you actually read the instructions on the more popular wine base concentrates, you'll notice that a lot of them still include fermenting with must (crushed fruit) included (don't worry – this will make more sense later when we walk through the actual process of making wine). Adding in whatever amount of crushed real fruit you can access helps lend that fuller, more nuanced (Woah! Am I getting too fancy here?) taste and body to the wine. For example, let's say you were able to pick a half or a quarter of what you need to make a true batch of from-the-fruit wine. But you really don't want to settle for a tiny batch, because really, the time investment isn't a lot different for a small one-gallon batch as it is for a three- or five-gallon batch. This is a very good time to order in a can of juice, use it as your liquid base, and ferment your smaller amount of fruit in it to add a boost of fresh flavor.

- **Give it a try just the way it is.** We all know how these online feedbacks and reviews go; one person's experience or perception can be completely opposite to another's, and there is *always* going to be a naysayer. There are plenty of people giving these bases great reviews and saying their wine came out very pleasingly. So, what of it? If you don't have the fruit, you just want to give it ago in a quick and easy way without a whole lot to lose, go ahead and *do it*. As I said, there is always the option to back-flavor. We're all about making home winemaking simpler and removing the roadblocks that more complex, lab-driven methods present. It's back to the basics, and grandpa wasn't afraid of a little trial!

Wine Making When the Mood Strikes

If you're anything like me, your wine-making ambitions and the time to make it don't always line up. Not unusually, I'll find the time to harvest the fruit without the rest of the time needed to follow it through the stemming, smashing, crashing and crushing processes. Sometimes I know that although I have a window to get a wine started one week, the following week is looking awfully muddled and finding the time to move through the next step is going to be tough. There is another issue that I frequently run into, especially with certain crops like berries: Crops that trickle in and don't ripen all at the same time (raspberries and blackberries that I'm foraging come to mind). The issue with these crops is that it's hard to get enough yield at one time to make a batch.

The thing about making wine in this modern age, an age where many of us might love the idea of homesteading and self-sufficiency (or not), but an age where most of us have to do something to pay the bills and are pressed in a hundred other directions (sports taxi, anyone?), is that we don't always have the *time* when the time is right. Fruits and berries ripen on their own schedule, selfishly disregarding the fact that our weekends are too jam-packed for those critical weeks of optimal harvest and the boss is flashing incredulous looks when you ask for days off for destemming and crushing. So while we might have access to some excellent local options, we often lack the opportunity at the opportune time. What then?

Well, the one good thing we can say for our modern living is that we've developed excellent long-term storage solutions, like freezing. Freezing is the perfect in-season solution to in-season time constraints. It is also the perfect solution to staggered harvests and limited determinate ripening (determinate referring to plants on which all the crops ripen at the same time). Frequently I will freeze fruits or berries in small batches until I have enough of a given berry to warrant putting the time into a large enough batch of wine. It's not uncommon for me to freeze a bucket full of grapes until I can get to them later (it's also not uncommon for me to pull out those grapes to thaw, open them up, find out they're really last year's elderberries and make jelly). Brain fumbles aside, freezing is a real first-world solution for me, and it should be for you, too, if life otherwise gets in your way.

If you do decide to freeze berries and fruits for future wine use, remove the stems and give them a wash, then drain for a while to dry and freeze them in whatever portions are most sensible for you. For making wine, I prefer to freeze in the largest bulk bags, Tupperware, or freezer-proof containers that I can fit, up to the amount needed for a single batch or in a few smaller batches until I can eventually make up enough of a store. For fruits like peaches and plums, it's easiest if you halve and pit them prior to freezing, which also makes it that much easier to deal with them when they come out. For things like grapes and berries, after destemming and washing, just freeze whole. They'll actually be easier to crush after thawing and will release their juices more easily, so taking them any further at this stage is just making unnecessary work for yourself. When you are ready to make your fruit into wine, remove your stash a few days ahead of time and thaw them under refrigeration. Make sure to thaw the fruit out all the way and let them sit out for a few hours to come to room temperature before making your wine so that you don't end up with problems getting your yeast started when the time comes.

All in all, it's nice to have some alternatives like those we've discussed here so that you always have a resource for playing and making your own homemade wines. Real wine is wine made from-the-fruit (or from-the-vegetable as the case may be). Juices and concentrates give some good alternatives, but really the best, most unique wine you'll make is that made from fresh ingredients that lend their own finer characteristics. Still, we shouldn't get so hung up that we let a lack of personal or local resources keep us from pursuing something of fun and interest to us. So, consider what we've talked about here. Think about the different options and strategies and figure out what works for you. Decide what is most available and workable to you personally and make a batch or three. Give it a try and see what you can create!

3

THE YEAST

Yeast is a major player when you're making wine. Without it, all you have is juice. If you start a search on yeasts for making wine, you'll soon find out that there are a whole lot of options out there; more types and varieties than you could ever imagine, all from what is, essentially, a very simple, naturally-occurring little organism. It's a quick and easy way to get overwhelmed and want to quit before you start, so let's see if we can make this part of the process a little less daunting.

THE ROLE OF YEAST IN WINE MAKING

The specific types of yeast that are used for baking, bread-making, and winemaking (Saccharomyces cerevisiae, if you want to get scientific about it, which we don't...too much), are what are known as "sugar-eating" yeasts. It's yeast's love of sweets that gives us the good stuff.

Yeasts can live and reproduce in environments both with and without oxygen. When that reproduction takes place in an environment that is essentially lacking oxygen, the resulting process is fermentation and the byproducts produced by the yeast are carbon dioxide and alcohol. Hence, in our case, wine.

To grow and thrive, yeast requires a handful of essentials: Warmth, nutrients, a food source (sugar, primarily, for our yeast), and moisture (in the form of water-based juice in the case of wine). In the absence of one or more of these factors, yeast doesn't really "die," as such, it really goes more into a state of hibernation and spore production (resulting in what is known as a "stuck" fermentation). This isn't something we have to concern ourselves with overly much, save to understand that we want to create the ideal conditions for our yeast to thrive and reproduce, and then create the environment that stops that reproduction before we turn the wine into vinegar. We also do not want to provide environmental factors that might restart the yeast and fermentation.

Taken down to the basics, this is how wine is made. The must, along with the dissolved sugar, water, and fruit juice, create both the base for the wine and the environment for the yeast. Given this "right" environment, the yeast then begins to multiply and reproduce. The yeast cells feed on the sugar and go into a phase of heavy reproduction. As they eat, they digest the sugar and convert it into those two byproducts, alcohol and carbon dioxide. The carbon dioxide bubbles up and eventually away and the alcohol remains.

The process of fermentation naturally stops when the yeast has "eaten" the bulk of the available sugars and nutrients. As this conversion process goes on, the environment created by the yeast becomes inhospitable to the yeast. Not only will the yeasts' source of food, sugar and nutrients be gone, but the concentration of alcohol in the new environment will be too high for the yeast to live. As the concentration of alcohol heads towards 14%, the yeast will stop reproducing, move through a state of dormancy, and eventually die. The level of alcohol that a specific strain of yeast can live in will vary by species, but typically yeasts can no longer live when the alcohol level reaches between 14 and 18 percent. Once all of this happens, fermentation essentially stops on its own and will result in a wine that is usually pretty "dry." A low level of sweetness will remain because there are still types of sugars present in the new wine (in much smaller quantities) that the yeast is not able to "feed" on and which the yeast cannot ferment. The level of natural sweetness or dryness that remains once fermentation ends depends a lot on the content of the fruit and produce to begin with; the characteristics and chemical makeup of the produce itself. Other factors including the recipe used and yeast strains also come to bear.

Although we promised to keep the process as simple and uncomplicated as possible in this book, and we're venturing dangerously close to science in this section, it is helpful to know a little bit about the process and life cycle of yeast in making wine. If you know just a little bit about how yeast works to turn fruity water into wine, you'll understand the basics of your part in it – what the wine needs you to give it, what environment it needs for the yeast to thrive, and how to avoid problems that might stop your wine dead in its tracks.

YEAST'S MOST COMFORTABLE CLIMATE

The climate in which we make our wine is a very important factor. What we're really talking about here is temperature. (Other climate factors, like humidity and moisture, really take care of themselves for the most part and so until we talk about end-stage bottled storage, it's not worth a real worry here).

All yeasts, whether for baking, brewing, or winemaking, are temperature sensitive. If they are too cold, they are slow, sluggish, and possibly even dormant; too hot and they die. At cold temperatures, yeasts do not multiply. They don't do a lot of anything. If your wine and must are below a favorable temperature threshold, the yeast will not proliferate, and rotting rather than fermentation will occur.

Temperatures that are in too high a range lend a different set of problems. At high temperatures, the issue is not that yeast will not act; it's that they will, basically, *over*react. When making wine, if conditions are even just a little too far towards the high-end of warm for an extended period of time, the yeast will ferment at too rapid a pace and, while the yeast will ferment the components, they will not create a particularly good-tasting wine. Flavor will not only suffer, but off-flavors will be produced that you do not want in your wine. The reason this happens is that in addition to yeast, wine must contains other enzymes, and sometimes even microorganisms. Under ideal conditions, the yeast is provided the right temperature and climate to thrive and outcompete these elements. When those conditions are off, these enzymes and microorganisms can get more of a hold and have the warmth they need to really take off, in which case they start giving off things that produce a whole other set of flavors to the wine. Not what we are going for.

What, then, is yeast's most comfortable temperature? What is the best temperature at which to ferment wine?

In answer to this question, you're apt to find a lot of different responses and I've seen some wide ranges but staying within a range in the low 70's (Fahrenheit) is best. Those who go in for more scientific and detail-regulated winemaking will say to go as low as 55 degrees for white wines, which benefit from a slower fermentation, but here you start to risk those problems relating to slow yeast growth and "stuck" fermentation (when the process basically stops before the fruit and juice becomes wine). Many – certainly not all – of these wine-makers will push red wines to a higher end of the spectrum, up towards 80 degrees, red wines being capable of managing and maintaining fermentation at a higher temperature.

At the end of the day, you are best off with a temperature in the well-accepted comfort zone, and that is widely accepted to be in the range of 70 to 75 degrees. The very well-respected home brewing and winemaking supply house EC Kraus, in the business for well over a half century, lists 72 degrees as the optimal temperature that home winemakers should strive for, noting that anything fairly constant in the range of 70 to 75 is reliable for a good result. It is also worth noting that fermentation and yeast activity changes by percentages once you move toward the higher end of recommended temperature ranges and above (keeping in mind that yeast can live at temperatures much, much higher than the desired 72). This is when those enzymes and microorganisms and that fast fermentation really take hold and produce off flavors. Thus, if you have to make a choice between selecting a location that might be a bit off from the ideal of 72, you are better off with a location with a temperature towards the lower end rather than a temperature that is likely to push temps much toward, or worse yet over, 80 degrees.

To bring this discussion back down to basics, what you need to know about fermentation temperature for good, cheap, easy wines is this:

- What is most comfortable to you is what is most comfortable to yeast, too. Seventy-two is a pretty comfortable place for you to sit in any season; the same is true for your yeast.
- Choose a location in your house where you don't mind having fermenting wine sticking around for about a month and a half. Keep in mind that especially early on, there will be odors (not necessarily bad, but definitely different smells than what are typical at home).
- Look for a place that is pretty consistent in temperature and that you can be reasonably assured will stay in the desired 70-75-degree range on most days. You want to avoid big fluctuations in temperature to either side, which can get yeast "stuck" and open doors for unwanted organisms.
- Be aware of microclimates in a room caused by drafts, heating, and cooling sources. Next to a drafty open door isn't a great spot; neither is a spot too close to a stove, or an oven that might significantly change the temperature.
- Consider that if you are making wine at different times of the year, what is an ideal space in one season might not be a good place at all in another, primarily for those reasons just mentioned.

A kitchen, of course, is one of the best places to ferment your wine because it is, obviously, nearby to all the resources you need and is ready to handle a mess (including, perhaps, an overflowing bucket left a little too full for bubbling first fermentation...not that I've ever done this [I certainly have] and not that it's fun [it certainly isn't], but at least it's in the kitchen). Of course, that is if you feel you have a space in your kitchen that won't be subject to cold or hotspots and fluctuations. Because kitchens frequently are, a lot of people find that a nearby room, like a dining room or pantry, is a more consistent place in which to brew. I've found that one of my best locations that is very steady in temperature is a closed closet just off my kitchen. If you're not sure what temperature your place of choice is, just stick a thermometer there for a few days and check it out as you get things ready. Take a look when the heater, oven, or air conditioner are on. It should give you a pretty good idea of what to expect for the next several weeks ahead, barring any extreme changes in weather. Site-selection isn't worth a lot of stress and I wouldn't lose sleep over a hint of an extra degree or two here and there, but it is worth it to put a bit of thought and planning into it for all your upcoming effort.

WHICH YEAST TO CHOOSE?

There are over 1500 species of yeast identified by man, existing in various habitats right now. That's 1500+ that we *know* about. They float in the air and they live in water, on plants and leaves, in soil and detritus, on fruits... In fact, there is, more than likely, wild yeast already living on your wine ingredients. Fed up through the process of making wine, these wild yeasts could initiate fermentation, multiply and grow, and maybe even produce a good, natural wine.

And maybe not. Maybe the yeast that's come in with you isn't such a good strain for making wine. Maybe it will be over-reactive. Or under-reactive. Or maybe it throws the wrong flavors and just doesn't produce a wine that tastes good. (In my family, we all have some pretty vivid memories of an aunt who went au-naturel with some local wild grapes, sans added sugar, with high hopes; it's probably the reason none of us tried making wine ourselves until we were in our thirties). And this, my friends, is why we use yeast of a more commercial nature when we make wine at home. It's just plain more reliable.

Now, we've already established that saccharomyces cerevisiae, the sugar-eating yeast, is the yeast that we use to make wine, breads, and brews. However, there are more than 700 strains of saccharomyces cerevisiae. Biologically speaking, these strains are only minor in difference, but the different strains do lend different qualities that make some maybe a little better than others for certain uses. They exhibit different characteristics such as alcohol tolerance, temperature tolerance, vigor and the ability to maintain extended fermentation, and the production of byproducts which lend to the aromatic and flavor profiles of the wines they produce.

There is great debate in wine-making circles and amongst research scientists who study these strains of so-called sugar-eating yeasts as to the significance of the impact that different strains have on the wines produced. It has also been said that even amongst those yeast strains that are mostly agreed upon as imparting something significant to wine, some specific benefit or attribute, those attributes are most prevalent while the wines are young, and tend to mellow out as wines age, thus becoming a less important factor over time and as the wine ages.

What does all of this mean for us as cheap and easy, uncomplicated home winemakers? It means there are many more options than we probably want to think about. So, let's see if we can take it down to just a few reliable basics.

In wine making, yeasts are selected for many reasons, but the primary among them is their reliability; their ability to reliably get started and established multiplying so as to out-compete any wild yeasts that are present (get the jump and do the job right), and their reliability to sustain fermentation throughout the entire process without dying off and leaving an only partially-completed fermentation. There are certainly other, finer points that come into play for commercial wineries and the more serious hobby winemakers, but these are the two main points yeast selection really comes down to, and all that we really need to most concern ourselves with as we select yeasts for simplified wine making.

What about bread yeast?

When most of us think of yeast, we think of bread yeast, or baker's yeast—the yeast we find in virtually any grocery store that is used for baking beautiful breads, buns, and doughs. So, what of it? Can't we just use bread yeast? What's the difference?

The fact is that there isn't an essential difference between baker's yeast and wine yeast. These are yeasts of the same species – all saccharomyces cerevisiae; all sugar-eating yeasts. The difference between a given wine yeast and bread yeast is that they are all just different strains of the same. Some people feel strongly that choosing just that right strain for its fine differences and characteristics is imperative; others feel that it's all a lot of overwhelming minutiae and it's easy to get caught up in it and stuck before you even start. The choice, really, is yours.

In the commercial wine-making trade, and certainly amongst wine-making supply and information publishing resources, you'll quickly find that to them, making wine with bread yeast is absolutely off-limits. Articles abound about why making wine with dedicated wine yeast is the only way you can go. What's interesting is that if you read beyond the articles and through the comments from people from all walks who are or have made wine, there is actually a lot of support for using bread/baker's yeast to make your homemade wine. Many people *are* doing it. Many people *have* done it and continue to choose bread yeast for fermenting wine. Generations ago bread yeast is what people had; what they used; what they enjoyed, with consistent success.

Why would anyone use bread yeast with so many great wine yeasts available?

I'm going to go on the record here in support of making wine with bread yeast. Yes, I'm going to put myself out there, come out of the dark and admit it:

"I use bread yeast to make my homemade wine."

I don't always, but often, I do. And here's why.

The bottom line? It works. It has worked. It continues to work, and my wines have been delicious.

The first wine I ever made was with our abundance of wild grapes, made with Frank Petersohn's very basic instructions and with a little light background reading from some homesteading- and back-to-basics-type resources like "Mother Earth News" articles. None of these resources really differed a lot from each other because they all followed a traditional, uncomplicated, clean-living process of fermentation without a lot of extraneous or complicated additives. They relied on good, old-fashioned knowledge and accessible ingredients, and none of them were afraid of using bread yeast. In fact, many recommended it.

I started out with bread yeast for a very simple reason: It was available to me. I knew what it was. It was easy to access on a moment's notice, didn't cost a lot, and in fact, I had it in my pantry since I make an awful lot of bread.

So, I made my first gallons of wine with bread yeast and it came out potent and delicious. It was a huge hit all-around. We shared with many friends and a few who (even though they had never made a drop of wine or brew in their lives, and had never been involved in making it with anyone else) insisted that I just "had" to make the next wine with wine yeast. Imagine how much better it would be with wine yeast! And so, the next year, I did. I was a good girl, playing by the rules, went online and bought myself what is touted as a good, solid, versatile wine yeast for the reds I was making and went to town.

I couldn't see any appreciable difference at all. The wine tasted virtually the same, The aroma of New England stone wall was just as prevalent and enjoyable in the wine made with my bread yeast as with the wine yeasts (my grapes grow largely along the stone walls of our property and it imparts a wonderful, earthy, down-home "nose" and nostalgia). Fermentation took off strongly each time I made my wine using bread yeast and remained steady throughout, following the timeline of the process that it should; the wine cleared beautifully.

As a matter of fact, the only time that I have had yeast fail me, resulting in an incomplete, over-sweet fermentation, was when I *did* follow the rules and used wine yeast. That's not saying it was necessarily because of wine yeast that the batch failed, or that bread yeast is better; it's only to say that, that was my experience (and it's an experience others report, too). And while I'm not here to argue against wine yeast, I do want to make the point that bread yeast has been a reliable component for me, and after some dabbling, it's what I've gone back to, and what I use on a regular basis.

To be fair, there could be other explanations for why wine yeast didn't work out for me some of those times. I'm sure there are. Chief among them is likely an issue of handling somewhere along the way. The yeast may have been stored in an area that was too warm. It may have been old. It may have been allowed to sit in an area of too-high humidity. It may have been left sitting for days in the dog days of summer on some shipping company loading dock; maybe the dockers used the box as a football and compromised the packaging. It's possible that I had something not quite right in my wine-making process – perhaps my must and water were too warm when I rehydrated the yeast before pitching it into the batch. Perhaps the temperature in the bucket was too high when I pitched it; perhaps the temperature was too high, too low, or allowed to fluctuate too much over the course of the first or second fermentation period. Maybe the strain of yeast I chose just wasn't quite up to the task of my particular fruit. Maybe it's simply a matter of me using bread yeast regularly and so my stock remains fresher because it is rotated through with more frequency (which seems unlikely, given that I'd purchased the wine yeast recently from an online supplier). Maybe the issue is that because I use a simplified, back-to-basics process to make my wine, I do not do all the testing and alchemy before I pitch my yeast. So who knows? Maybe when you're not testing things like brix and Ph and adding in additives like potassium or sodium metabisulfite, yeast energizers, speedy bentonite, pectin enzymes, wine conditioners and others, maybe then bread yeast is a better performer.

One other reason that is often cited by winemakers who are using bread yeast is availability. Sure, online options have really opened doors to many of us and wine and brew supplies from actual, dedicated wine-making suppliers are easier than ever to access, even for those of us in remote locations. There are a surprising number of people on forums joining in the discussion saying they live in a country or location that is essentially "dry", whether for cultural or religious reasons, and where the sale of supplies for producing alcohol is restricted, and therefore baker's yeast is their only option...but alas, it hasn't proved a bad one. Actual brick-and-mortar supply stores are relatively few and far between, though. Almost any one of us can run downtown to the local grocer and buy a few packets of fresh baker's yeast without too much planning and waiting. To sum up one commenter's sentiment on the matter, the wine in the bottle is better than the fruit that rots. If it takes bread yeast to make it, so be it.

Cost is another factor that a lot of people who use bread yeast cite as a reason that they choose to use it. It is a valid point and bread yeast that you buy locally is almost definitely the cheapest yeast you'll come by. Usually, a triple-envelope pack of bread yeast is only a little cheaper than a similar count of wine yeast envelopes. Unless you have a local walk-in supply shop, though, you'll probably have to add something for the cost of shipping to that price, which bumps the price of your wine yeast up a little more. How much more depends on where you're buying it from. It's up to you to decide where you want to draw the line on the cost of your yeast and how much of a factor price will be for you. For cheap and easy winemaking, I'd have to say the cheapest route is most likely to be regular active dry yeast (ADY) packets from the neighborhood grocery store.

Finally, we come to the confusion factor. This is another very real reason why a lot of people will choose to go with simple, basic bread yeast for making wine. The list of wine yeast options seems endless.

There are many different yeast brands, and within those brands, there are numerous types and strains of wine yeast. Some have pretty names. Some have something akin to reference numbers. There are lists and charts and plenty of advice and recommendations designed to help you choose the right yeast for your project. It can all be very overwhelming. And so sometimes, when you just want to get down to it, to play and put your hand to producing something delicious, you decide not to spend that time combing through all the infinite opinions about *exactly* which strain is just right, and you pitch some cheap and easy bread yeast and get on with it. And that is okay, too.

At the end of the day for me the argument is no argument at all. I enjoy my wines. I've had success with bread yeast, so I use it. As more than one commenter in the great debate has said, they have friends, often homesteader types (but certainly not always), and many have successfully, enjoyably, and repeatedly chosen bread yeast. They make their wine with baker's yeast and they enjoy the outcome; and shouldn't that be all that matters? Isn't the enjoyment of the product what wine making is all about?

The argument for wine yeast

I don't deny that dedicated wine yeasts can be good. I realize I have just spent a lot of time arguing the case for bread yeast, but there are equally good reasons why using a "real" wine yeast might be the route you choose to go. It's not a matter of one against the other. It's a matter of choice and options.

While a generic yeast is apt to produce a wine you'll enjoy and be perfectly happy with, wine yeasts are one place where you can take that same shared recipe, twist and tweak and experiment with it and make it something truly your own. "Award-winning" is what a lot of wine yeast proponents say. But then, if just "enjoyable" is what you're after, an "award-winning" yeast strain probably doesn't matter so much to you.

There are a number of reasons that the experts feel that a carefully-selected strain of wine yeast is your best choice:

• **Favorable byproduct production.** In addition to alcohol, when fruit ferments into wine, other products are produced such as enzymes, oils, and acids. These all contribute to the flavor profile of the finished wine. The very specific yeasts developed for winemaking select for favorable byproduct production.

• **Lower alcohol levels.** Bread yeast is expected to produce wines with alcohol contents in the lower range. Experts agree that baker's yeast can easily achieve an alcohol level of eight to nine percent but may begin to struggle much over ten percent. That could potentially be a problem if the wine is not yet completely fermented, and therefore as the process runs out, the wine produced may be sweeter than desired. It is not, however, much of an issue as far as the safety of the wine because eight percent alcohol is considered a good, safe, lower threshold for wine. In fact, many commercial winemakers are producing wines with even lower alcohol levels (in the range of 7 to 7.5%). Why? Because the market is demanding it. People are really coming to like lower-alcohol wines and the market is responding to it.

As a point of reference, 10 to 14% is considered the average range for alcohol in wines, both homemade and commercial. Reds like Merlot and Cabernet trend towards 13.5 to 14% alcohol. Dry white wines usually fall into the same range, while sweeter, lighter wines like Moscato typically have lower percentages of alcohol, usually 10% or under. Fourteen percent is considered about the max that you want to reach in a wine. When you start to exceed that, you start losing the wine palate all together and start producing something that tastes much more like hard alcohol. What this all means is that it's up to you to decide how important producing a high-alcohol wine is to you. However, you do need to keep in mind that the selected yeast is only *one* factor in alcohol production – an awful lot of it has to do with the fruit and what it brings to the batch (which also varies by year, growing conditions, and other factors). This is precisely why we have "good" wine years and not-as-good wine years. It also has to do with other factors in a recipe including how much sugar is added and so on.

One thing I will add to the point here is this: I don't know what the alcohol content of any of the wines I have ever made is, because I don't do the chemistry. I'm happy to go through the process and see what comes out, and not too worried about the percent alcohol; I just want to enjoy a simple, tasty country wine. I can say that the first time we tried our first homemade wine was an education, and we learned to take some care. It went down easily and perked us up quickly. There was plenty of alcohol content, whatever it was. My husband (no stranger to a few hearty glasses of wine), dubbed it a "one-mason-jar wine." (Yes, he was drinking from a mason jar. I'm not sure why, but even a guy his size with a good tolerance level felt four cups was a good upper limit for a long evening.) And so, I think our bread-yeast produced a wine with a plenty high alcohol content without any trouble.

• **Clearing the wine.** Bread yeast is also reported to produce a wine that does not clear easily, and hence produces a somewhat hazy wine. This is mostly aesthetics anyway but for me, I've just not found it to be a problem. Wine that does not clear is one of the more common difficulties of home winemaking, but there are often steps you can take to help the process along. That's somewhat beside the point here, but it should be noted that using wine yeast, or one yeast over another, doesn't necessarily guarantee difficulty clearing, or ensure that haziness will not be an issue. Moreover, most of the time the process completes itself and the wine clears nicely anyway).

These are considered to be the major arguments in favor of using wine yeast as opposed to a bread or baker's yeast in home wine production.

If wine yeast feels like a safer bet for you, you should most definitely feel very comfortable in doing so. If you feel like you're not opposed to making wine with bread yeast, but it just seems safer to go with wine yeast, then that is exactly what you should do. If you feel like maybe making a batch with this, and maybe a batch with that, and compare and contrast, those are great options, too.

Tips on Choosing a yeast

Truth be told, whether you decide on using wine yeast or bread yeast, or mixing it up as the mood strikes, it's always a good idea to compare and contrast and do a little note-taking for future reference because believe me, much as we all think we'll remember the finer points, we won't. For all yeasts, including bread yeast but most particularly for wine yeasts, you'll have a few decisions to make when selecting your yeast.

For bread yeasts the decisions aren't many because the yeast itself is really the same strain across the board; you don't really get a host of strains to choose from. You do get to choose the brand and where you purchase it from, however. You shouldn't stress too much over this. If you're comfortable grabbing up what you come by in the grocery, do it. Simplification is probably the best reason to use bread yeast.

Here are some tips for selecting bread yeast for making wine:

• **Choose a reliable brand.** I personally like Fleischmann's. It's been the most reliable for me both for baking bread and for making wine. But there are certainly other good yeast brands out there and depending on where you shop and what they carry, you may have more limited brand options.

• **Choose active dry yeast** over Rapid Rise™, bread machine, or instant yeast. Rapid Rise™ is actually a brand-specific yeast, meaning it is a brand name. It is Fleischmann's name for their instant yeast; basically, instant yeast, Rapid Rise™, and any type of bread machine yeast are all the same thing. They are designed to act fast and cut down on proofing and rising time. It's a great thing if you want to make great bread in short time. When we make wine, we don't want a more convenient and fast-acting yeast; we want one with stamina that will go the distance. And so that is why I stay away from any form of instant yeast and go with traditional, slower-acting active dry yeast (what most people would think of as "regular yeast".

And now my caveat, in the interest of accessibility and open-minded wine yeast selection. I have read comments from people who use Rapid Rise™ or instant yeast. They say it works a charm. If it's worth a try for you, go right ahead and do it. I'd be interested in hearing about it, really. It just seems a dicier selection to me, knowing that its function is designed more for fast production than sustained production (I always think of it as the sprint or fast middle-distance run opposed to the cross country or marathon.)

• **Buy it somewhere you trust the handling.** There are probably a fair number of people who don't concern themselves with sellers/suppliers as much as I do, and that's okay. There are probably plenty of intelligent arguments in support of product protection due to superior packaging processes these days, but I do know that I've bought yeast in lots of places, online and off, from many different sellers, and it seems the better sellers provide a better product, even when the brands and types are the same. I have to think this is a matter of popularity and stock rotation from high turnover, and also care in storing and handling. And so, I try to buy my yeast at the places where I think the stock is more likely to be turned over more often and therefore has less age on it, and where I think the storage conditions are less stressful, with responsible handling. Go the more frequented grocer. Buy from the same seller online if you can, if their product has shown quality and vigor in the past.

A couple of these tips for selecting wine yeasts are the same as for bread yeasts. There's just more to consider because there's a much wider array of choices.

- **Go with brand reliability.** A handful of wine yeast manufacturers have risen to the top of the game through years of research and development, and they've produced some very good reliable products. If you're taking the bother to use a wine yeast, it only makes the most sense to go with a trusted brand.

- **Buy from a reputable supplier.** This is the business who you trust to provide a fresh, quality product and handle it well. Especially when buying online from sites like Amazon, you'll find hundreds of sellers. But a lot of these are often resellers and who knows how direct their supply is. If I'm going to bother buying wine yeast, even if the cost is a little more, I'm going to buy from a wine and/or brew supply company. These are the people I trust to keep a quality product in stock and handle it well. These are also the people who can best help you match your yeast selection to your wine project. Here in the U.S., I've found EC Kraus and Midwest Supplies to be good. There are several others who also specialize in wine and brewing supplies, and many of these reputable companies can also be found selling on platforms like Amazon and other large online retailers.

- **Don't reinvent the wheel.** So many people have made so many wines using so many different fruits and types of produce, and have put so much time into searching out the right yeast for each purpose, there's no need to reinvent the wheel here. Do a little searching. Google things like "yeast for wild grape wine [insert fruit or produce of choice here]". At least in the beginning, do yourself a favor and follow the lead of those who've come before you. (Later in this book you will find some specific recommendations, too.)

- **Feel Free to experiment.** Following the lead of others doesn't

mean that you don't get to play, too. All those people out there
with their fantastically delicious, quirky little wines got there
by daring to play around a little. Start manageably, but over
time, do spread your wings. Once you get more of a feel for
making wine and for using different yeasts, then try some
experimentation to make your wine your own.

- **Match your yeast to your produce.** When you do start doing
  some searching, you'll notice quickly that winemakers
  consider certain yeasts to be *the* yeast "for" certain grapes or
  certain fruits. Either the flavor profile they impart is ideal, or
  they have been known to perform well given the specific
  nutrient and sugar profiles of the produce in question. This
  often comes down to grape varietals amongst more traditional
  winemakers, but there are a lot of charts and lists out there for
  other fruit types and wild grapes and berries, too. These are a
  good place to start. With more "country" style wines, it can
  sometimes be tough to get exact recommendations and so in
  that case, choose a fruit or grape that is most like the fruit or
  grape you are working with and choose a yeast recommended
  for that similar fruit.
- **Consider what style of wine you'd like to produce.** What do
  your tastes in wine trend toward? Dry? Semi-dry? Full-bodied?
  Sweet? Light? There are yeasts that are better suited to produce
  each of these over another. Looking back to the lists and charts,
  select for the criteria you would like to produce in your end
  product.
- **Consider the flavor profile of the yeast.** Each strain of yeast is
  known to produce slightly different flavors in the wine they
  produce. For example, a yeast may be said to produce a fruity,
  smoky, or buttery wine. If there are particular flavors you think
  you'd like, you can base part of your yeast selection on this
  factor.
- **Choose a sturdy performer.** For fruit and wild wines, it is
  often recommended to choose a yeast that is up to dealing with
  some of the more common issues and problems faced in

winemaking – consider it a sort of prevention or insurance against those challenges. Choose a strain that is generally known to work even in less-than-ideal circumstances. Look for a strain that can handle temperature, nutrients, and pH at lower levels — especially if you plan not to add in additional additives.

- **Think about ease of use.** In this case, we're talking about ease of use in terms of performance. Some yeasts are just known to ferment more quickly; to reliably take hold and run that steady race well and easily. Other yeasts are considered slower or moderate fermenters. There are reasons people choose these yeasts and it has to do with character development. However, those slower, more moderate fermenters can be temperamental, and are more likely to stop or get "stuck." They're not always the best yeasts for beginners, especially if there could be some slightly stressing production or environmental factors. On yeast profile charts, what I'm calling "ease of use" (because it's easier for you if you can reasonably rely on its fermentation ability) will often be listed as "Fermentation Speed", or you might otherwise find this information in a description where a yeast might be described as a "slow fermenter", "fast fermenter", and so on.

- **Wide-spectrum yeasts save you money.** Among the two major wine yeast brands discussed in this book, each has a yeast that is considered all-purpose and reliable. It's a good idea to consider just sticking with the more general, all-purpose types, which will usually save you money because when you buy yeast you often have to buy multiple packets. They may be sold in bunches of five or ten, especially online. If you use three or four different types of yeast for four different batches of wine, you can easily end up buying 30 or 40 packets, 99% of which will probably expire and weaken before you ever get to use them, and thus become a costly waste.

All of this considered, it is also important to remember that yeast is only one factor. You can research and select for those characteristics that are important to you, but you can't expect a yeast to turn your fruit into something that it's not. Yeast selection is a matter of match-making. You're making the best match between your fruit and the yeast to produce the wine with the elements you favor. A good match will make a good, probably great, wine. An okay match will still most likely produce a good, and often great, wine. And then, what's considered "good" and "great" are subjective anyway. I mention this only to give you the confidence to try it and know that either way, the odds are still in your favor! (Remember – I'm here making great wine with a generic yeast!)

Some Good, Reliable Basic Wine Yeast Recommendations for Beginners

Now that we've brought the topic to a more complex level let's see if we can bring it back down to a much more simple, navigable one.

The toughest part of using wine yeast is in choosing one from the many. Not only do you have different strains of yeast to choose from, but you have different brands, too. Of course, those different brands don't always call the same strain by the same name. It's not like saying, "I want creamy peanut butter," and deciding, "I'll get Jif instead of Skippy," because in this case Jif is going to call their creamy peanut butter smooth and Skippy is going to call their peanut butter something obscure, like PBt11-119. If you set off trying to "shop" your yeast by actual scientific strain name, the cross referencing will be enough to make you want to give up altogether and rip your hair out in the process. Instead, just put your energy into getting to know a few by their brand and names or reference numbers.

There are at least four major players in the brand arena and they pretty much offer the same things, but a couple tend to stand out over the others. Those two are Lalvin and Red Star. (Wyeast and White Labs are the other two big players, but this is sometimes a geographical matter.) To add to the confusion, Lalvin goes by different names in different countries — you'll often come across "Lallemand" instead, depending on the home-base of the resource or supplier; this could be true of other suppliers, too. Both companies have also decided to play around with some of the strain names, so older but excellent articles and resources sometimes have them listed by a different name. You can still usually find them by these older names as most books and web resources will not be updated with the name changes.

Red Star and Lalvin are fairly accessible through wine and brew suppliers and tend to be the most talked about, so, for the most part, we'll base our discussion on these two brands.

Among the most recommended common, reliable, and user-friendly yeasts for home winemakers are:

Red Star brands:

- **Premier Classique:** Red Star's Premier Classique was known for a long time as **Montrachet**. It is easily the most highly recommended wine yeast if the experts are asked to choose just one. It is almost a stand-alone above both brand and strain differentiation. It has the reputation of being the "all-purpose" of wine yeasts and is well known for ease-of-use. It is considered a very good yeast for almost any type of grape or fruit, neutral in flavor, and known to let the flavors of the fruit itself take center stage. It is a vigorous yeast that is a capable and reliable performer under most acceptable wine fermentation conditions. If it has a drawback, it would be that it does not offer up much in the way of flavor nuance or unique aroma, but winemakers and suppliers agree: If you don't know what yeast to use, or you are getting a headache just trying to decide, *use Red Star Premier Classique (Montrachet).*
- **Cote des Blanc:** (Also known as **Epernay II**) Cote des Blanc is a good yeast for grapes and fruits that will produce a "white" type wine but can be used in "reds" as well and imparts more fruity flavors to both. It is often recommended for the lighter,

whiter fruits, and for fruits in general. Cote des Blanc is especially recommended for apple wine. It is a slower fermenting yeast, can be a bit more temperature-sensitive, and usually produces a sweeter wine.

- **Premier Rouge:** (AKA **Pasteur Red** or **Red Pasteur**) Premier Rouge is considered ideal for any type of red wine and known as a strong fermenter, less apt to cause troubles. It is good for any of the heavier, darker grapes and berries, and is also a popular recommendation for wild produce, including grapes, blackberries, raspberries, and elderberries.
- **Premier Blanc:** (AKA **Pasteur Blanc**) Premier Blanc is known as a vigorous, reliable white-wine producer (think a bit of a more rigorous and safer version of Cote des Blanc). If you like the idea of Cote des Blanc but are scared off by its slower fermentation, this might be a good choice. Definitely note, though, that Premier Blanc produces a dryer, less sweet wine than Cote, owing to its increased activity level. While you might choose it because you can count on its reliability a little more, it might not be ideal if you wanted that sweeter fruity flavor. It is recommended for harder fermentation starts, fermenting white-type wines under less ideal circumstances, and for dryer ciders, whites, meads, and dryer fruit wines, including dry apple wines. It will also tolerate fermentation temperatures in the higher range more easily. (Tip: With this and other dry-producing but vigorous and reliable yeasts, keep in mind that if you are concerned you might have a tough time fermenting, go with the more rigorous and reliable dry-producer; you can always choose to back-sweeten a wine later.)

Lalvin yeasts:

- **K1-V1116:** (AKA **Montpellier**) This strain with a less-fun and -fancy name than Red Star (which is just typical of Lalvin brands), is comparable to Red Star's Cote des Blanc, in that is a good general choice for a white-type wine. What is has over

Cote des Blanc is that it is known as a more vigorous yeast, capable of dominating in a batch and fermenting in less ideal circumstances, including in low-nutrient environments. It's a good white-type wine choice when you don't want to add additional additives and yeast nutrients. It enjoys high user reviews and is noted for bringing out the freshness in white grapes and fruits like apples, pears, and peaches.

- **RC-212:** (AKA **Bourgovin**) Bourgovin is a good choice if you are looking to produce a full-bodied red wine with spicy notes and flavors. It is noted as producing aromas of ripe berry and pepper. It is considered a moderate fermenter, capable and reliable, but just a little more of a challenge.

- **EC-1118:** (AKA **Champagne** or **Prisse de Mousse**) This yeast is actually named after the Champagne region of France where it was isolated and developed, and not because it is a yeast specifically for making champagnes. That being said, it is considered to be *the* yeast for making champagne and sparkling wines. Bubbly wines, however, are not all that it can produce. In fact, if Lalvin is credited with an "all-purpose" wine yeast, this would be it. It has vigor and stamina. It establishes easily and easily out-competes wild yeast strains, so it is another good option for winemakers who want an additive-free wine. It can be used in either red or white wine production. It is neutral in flavor and aroma production, much like Montrachet, and showcases the fruit or produce. It is a top choice for wines made from late-harvest grapes and produce, as well ice wines. This yeast ferments well across a very wide temperature range and does well at the higher end of the temperature range (accepted as quite reliable in a range of 80-85^{0}F and some claim as high as 95F degrees). It is also a first-choice yeast for reviving wine in stuck fermentation or making wine under less-than-optimal conditions. When making wine during warm summer conditions, or when conditions can be less reliably controlled at lower temperatures, this is definitely a yeast to consider.

CHART: FAST-REFERENCE YEAST SELECTION

Yeast Name	Fermentation Vigor	Reliability	Temperature Range Tolerance	Produce Partners	Flavor & Aroma Profile	Comparable Commercial Wine Styles	Notes
Bread or Baker's Yeast	Good to Very Good	Moderately High	Good-Normal	All	Neutral under good conditions	N/A	An easy-to-access, cheap, all-around option
Premier Classique (Montrachet)	Very Good	High	Good-Normal	All	Neutral	N/A	Highest recommend-ation of experts; all-purpose; neutral base for any fruit or flavor
Cote des Blanc	Good but Slow	Moderate-Moderately High	Okay-Below normal; more temperature-sensitive	Lighter, whiter fruits, apples	Fruity	Sweeter white wines; Riesling; Chardonnay; Mead	Tends to produce sweeter wines but temperature sensitivity makes it more challenging
Premier Rouge	Very Good	High	Okay-Normal, but low-end sensitive	Wild grapes, Elderberry, Raspberry, Blackberry	Develops flavor of fruit used	Heavy Red Wines; Pinot's, Syrah, Cabernet	Reliable; helps bring out more subtle fruit flavors and weak and/or sub-optimally ripened fruits
Premier Blanc	Very Good	High	Very good-Above Normal; High-end temp range friendly	Lighter fruits; apples; meads	Neutral	Dry White Wines and Dry Ciders; Sauvignon Blanc	A more reliable yeast for white wine production but produces dryer, less sweet white wines
K1-V1116	Very Good	High	Very good-Above Normal	Fresh fruits, juice concentrates, peaches,	Neutral, fresh; develops flavors of fruit used	Sauvignon Blanc, Chenin Blanc	Performs well in low-nutrient environments; good base for developing

58

				white grapes, apples, pears			light fruit flavors
RC-212	Good	Moderate	Good-Normal	Dark grapes and dark berries	Ripe berry, spice, pepper	Burgundy, Pinot Noir, Full-bodied Red wines	Known for full flavor extraction and making the most of all that a fruit can give
EC-1118	Very Good	High	Very good-Above Normal	All fruits; late-harvest fruits; ice wine fruits	Neutral	Champagne and Sparkling wines; Red or white wines	Lalvin's all-purpose yeast; usable for both red and white wine styles; a good yeast for stuck fermentation; good when environment and temperature conditions are unreliable

STORING AND KEEPING YEAST

Today yeast is processed and packaged using techniques that generally guarantee them a pretty long shelf life. Nevertheless, yeast is a live organism and those organisms will begin to lose their vigor and eventually die off over time. It will also become stressed and inactive before its time if it is not handled and stored well. Given the importance of yeast to your wine, it's also important to make sure you do your part in keeping it as strong and vigorous as it can be while it waits.

Yeast is not hard to keep but there are a few optimal conditions for storage and handling you'll want to ensure. If you follow these few tips for yeast handling, storage, and use, you can be pretty well assured that your wine will be successful, or leastwise that issues will be much less likely to be caused by the yeast. That's a big deal because yeast really is one of your very top players. So, how best to store and keep your yeast?

- **Keep dry yeasts cool and dry.** The most popular and easily obtained yeasts are the freeze-dried, granulated version that come in small, sterile packaging that has been vacuum-sealed and designed to keep out moisture. For the most part (unless otherwise indicated), this is what we are talking about when we talk about yeast usage and storage. For dry yeast, cool, dry storage is the name of the game. By cool, normal room-temperature dry storage (a cabinet or cupboard, for example) is fine. Kept this way, dry yeast can be reliably stored for up to a year.

- **Avoid storage areas with potential temperature stress.** What you would most want to avoid in terms of temperature is storing your yeast in an area or environment that might grow too warm, such as in summer, or if the area is too close to a heat source. A cabinet above the oven, for example, isn't a great place to keep yeast. If storage temperatures creep upwards in the 70-degree range or beyond, that's a potential for activation and a stress that your yeast just doesn't need.

- **Refrigerate to extend yeast life.** Yeast can also be kept in a refrigerator, and even a freezer, although there are sources saying that freezing is a bad idea because it can harm the cell walls of the yeast, and therefore decrease the amount of viable yeast in a package. Lalvin has come forward saying that while they formerly recommended *not* freezing their yeast, after extensive experimentation and with today's good packaging, they have found no harm to yeast due to freezing, and that in fact, it performed better than yeast kept at room temperature. Kept refrigerated or frozen, yeast is said to be viable for up to two years.

- **Always refrigerate open bulk jars and liquid yeast.** Most of us won't be buying yeast in bulk-sized jars. Packets are more convenient and easier to keep reliably (and ideally pre-measured in a recipe-ready standard size). It is possible, though, especially if you are a bread-baker planning to use bread yeast, that you might opt to use yeast from a jar. If for whatever reason you are using yeast from a jar, know that its exposure to air and moisture through normal use makes it a little more vulnerable to unviability, so it should always be kept in a refrigerator when not out for use. When you do use it, measure out only what you need and return the rest of the jar to the refrigerator right away. Likewise, liquid yeast always requires refrigeration as well (even prior to opening).

- **Use bulk packages within 4 to 6 months.** Owing to the same reasons of exposure, bulk jars and packages do not have the shelf life, even in the refrigerator, of vacuum-sealed, lined packets. Red Star recommends using any open bulk jars of yeast within four to six months and keeping them only in an air-tight container, well-sealed.

- **Discard open packages.** Any open packet of yeast should just be thrown away, because those protective packaging qualities are lost once the package is open. Really, a packet of yeast is the smallest measure of yeast you should be using so this shouldn't be much of an issue, but it's worth knowing that it's not worth a few coins' value to try and keep an open package of yeast.

- **Stock rotation matters.** It's not the first time you've heard it in this book; the sellers and the rate of turnover, the amount of yeast they go through in the normal course of sales, matters. Let's remember that yeast is only considered good for two years (according to Red Star) from the manufacture date. You don't need all of your yeast's active life to be "lived" in a warehouse or on a store shelf because they only sell a packet or two per year.

- **Got a "use by" date?** Knowing how long *you* have kept a packet of yeast around, even if it is within its accepted one-year window, only tells half the story. As just mentioned, you can't always know how long that yeast has been in the stockroom of the seller. Yeast manufacturers will usually print either a date of manufacture or a "use by" date on the packaging. So, measure your time not from your date of purchase, but from the date of manufacture, or use it before the "use by" date has come and gone. Check dates before you plan to use the yeast (preferably with enough time to replace it if necessary!) and throw out anything that is too old, or too iffy.

- **Definitely discard compromised packages.** Look over your packets before use, too. If they seem punctured, slit, cut, or otherwise opened or compromised, if they seem "squishy," like air has been getting into something previously unopened, throw them out. It's just not worth going through all the effort of making your wine and finding out that a $2 packet of yeast was questionable.

- **Air and Oxygen are the big enemies.** What is a bigger danger than temperature is air and oxygen. Lalvin reports that in their trials, air was a much bigger factor than temperature fluctuations ever were. This is the primary reason why keeping any open packets or bulk packages for much more than six months, is a bad idea.

- **Don't stock too far ahead of yourself.** At the end of the day, considering the ease of access for good yeast and the fact that there's not usually much of a price break buying in bulk, it just doesn't seem like you gain a lot by stocking up too far ahead. Rather, I am of the opinion that it's wise to plan for one or two purchases per season or wine-making year so that you don't end up overspending on shipping, but so that you also keep your yeast young and fresh. Further, although instructions on how to "test" your yeast for viability aren't too hard to find, I'd argue that if in doubt, you're just better off spending a bit on a more sure-bet and new yeast. Gallons of good wine depend on it; it's just not worth the chance. My recommendation would be to estimate what kind and how much yeast you'll need for a season, make at least some of your selection a versatile strain like plain old bread yeast or an all-purpose Montrachet, buy a little more than you think might be necessary from a reputable source and then, rather than trying to keep it into early toddlerhood, buy fresh and new each year.

While there's been a lot discussed here in regard to yeast, the subject really isn't as complicated as it seems. Perhaps it's more accurate to say that the subject of yeast and wine making is as complicated as you want it to be. We've looked at some good, realistic, cheap, and manage-able options for wine yeast, from bread yeast to some reliable favorites, and some good, basic storage and handling. In the upcoming chapter we'll look at a few final considerations before we move on to the process itself.

4

A FEW FINAL DETAILS PRIOR TO THE PROCESS

There are a few other things worth talking about before we move onto the actual process (and recipes) of making cheap, easy wine at home. Consider this chapter a "collect all" for things that are worth mentioning but would be muddying the waters if talked about elsewhere.

CHEMICALS AND ADDITIVES

"By the book" winemakers use a lot of chemicals and additives in making their homemade wines. There's a basis for it, as it all serves a purpose. The method we employ does not get into this end of things because we are looking toward a much simpler, more natural, inexpensive way to make wine. It's one that doesn't add a lot of potential irritants and sensitivity-inducing elements like additional sulfites to the wine. I've counted upwards of seven *categories* of wine additives on top wine-making supply sites. That's just the categories, not including the list of additives that falls under each of those categories.

As said, there is a purpose to each of these additives, but I can tell you first-hand, as can many other homestead and country winemakers, that you *can* make great wine that preserves well without them.

Looking for the simplest, cleanest wine I can make, I don't bother with any of them to speak of. The argument for using them is that you're risking your wine by not protecting it with agents to kill the wild yeasts and organisms; with agents to condition the wine just so; with agents to stop the fermentation process; with agents to clear the wine, and so on, and so forth. While that's not untrue, it's also not entirely true. All winemaking has a risk of failing, with and without chemicals and additives. If this were not true, wine-making sites and forums wouldn't have a need for so many articles and endless forum discussions on how to fix problems that, in theory, should have been prevented with proper timing and use of chemicals to begin with.

What we need to keep in mind is that the process of making wine is a natural one. It was happening all on its own long before human beings ever got involved. Natural fermentation addresses those processes that these additives are designed to prevent and treat, all on its own. A good wine recipe will balance your fruits and flavors. The fermentation process will stop on its own as the yeast converts water into wine and builds an environment in which yeast can no longer survive. Good, basic temperature and environmental control will give your yeast a head start and will allow your yeast to outcompete the wild-card yeasts. Clearing is a natural part of the process that tends to happen well on its own (and even a cloudy wine is more of an aesthetic issue, and is only minorly a flavor issue; it is one of the reasons the old-timers used to decant their wines through a piece of fine cloth). A fair number of these additives are used for aesthetics that, while they might make a difference in something like the color of the wine over time, don't do a lot for things like flavor and have only become issues because some circles have moved more toward the idea of having to produce something that rivals the big houses. It brings to mind that "award-winning" sentiment again. It's reminiscent of a level of snobbery often associated with wine enjoyment, and, unfortunately, it has turned more than one person well off the idea of ever trying to make a homemade wine they can be proud of. I prefer the sentiment of Frank Petersohn: *"How the heck do you think your grandfather did it?"*

All this being said, and remembering that with or without additives, winemaking at heart is a natural process with its own set of controls, and sometimes things do go sideways, even for winemakers who are very much by-the-book. It is for this reason that I feel a few of these additives might be worth knowing about should a problem arise, as more of a troubleshooting fallback than anything. I won't speak about too many here for the simple reason that I rarely, if ever, use wine additives at all. If you are inclined to get into more of a detailed and designed wine, you'd be better off doing more research with entities with more knowledge and experience with them. Those that have been included here are the very basics that are easier to use and can address a couple of the more common problems that creep up in winemaking. I would usually look to these if I felt I needed to address an issue either retroactively, or proactively with a type of wine or fruit that I've struggled with in the past.

YEAST NUTRIENTS, TANNINS, AND ACID BLENDS

Yeast nutrient can be confusing because it can almost give the impression that it *is* yeast or that it *has* to be used. It is not. It does not.

Yeast nutrient is different than yeast. It is not a combination, and it does not take the place of yeast in winemaking. It can be used with any type of yeast because it simply is a supplemental nutrient booster for the must; think vitamins or supplements for yeast. Nutrients vary by company, but most will be based in Diammonium Phosphate (DAP), a salt which increases acidity and is intended to deliver more nitrogen to the wine. Opinions vary on how much and when to use the nutrient, but if you're just following a simple and easy process such as ours, and not getting into the chemistry of testing and balancing pH, and so on, it's probably best to look to it as a troubleshooter for when you feel fermentation might be getting too slow or stuck. That is a time you might want to add in a small amount of yeast nutrient to give things a boost. The risk of using nutrient when a must doesn't really need it is that the wine can go too far to the side of acid and then produce vinegar-type flavors that you most definitely don't want (unless you really like salad dressing).

Opting for the cleanest, most natural wine I can make with as little cost and interference as possible, I have never used yeast nutrient to date. Mr. Petersohn said he'd used it at times in his winemaking, and then stopped entirely, hadn't used it for years, and hadn't needed it. Many of today's winemakers are routinely using yeast nutrient as a recipe ingredient. Others will use it depending on the type of fruit or grape in use and the fruit's reputed nutrient content. As discussed here earlier, others use yeast nutrient retroactively as a way to fix a problem.

There are some middle-ground solutions and preventions, too. Andy Connelly, writing for *The Guardian* on home winemaking, suggests a cup of strong black tea made with regular tap water and a healthy dose of lemon juice (the juice of one lemon), which he adds as a natural yeast nutrient (his recipe is for an approximately one-gallon batch of wine, and so you would use roughly this amount per gallon in your batch). Black tea also has the advantage of being rich in tannins, another additive winemakers sometimes use, but which occurs naturally enough in dark fruits and berries.

There are other fruits that can be used to naturally provide the nutrients that additive yeast nutrient is designed to deliver and can either be used to bolster nutrients naturally or may, in fact, be added as flavor ingredients with the added benefit of providing natural yeast nutrient. Raisins fit this bill well. Older recipes very frequently include raisins and it is in part as a nutrient for the yeast, but also as a source of body for the wine that improves the "mouth feel" of the finished product. This helps smooth the harsh edges of some wines and helps flavors linger on the tongue, making them more detectable. Do note that raisins can sometimes add a caramelized taste to the wine, which is more notable in some wines than others (light and white wines in particular); white or golden raisins are equally good options that have less effect on the flavor.

Citric acid or acid blend is another common ingredient and additive in wine recipes of today, and one which has a very simple natural "substitute" (as ironic as it may be to be suggesting real fruit as a substitute for an engineered ingredient that we got from nature to begin with). Citric acid is easily introduced with the addition of citrus juices (as one might have guessed). Lemons are the most common, reliable, and versatile choice in terms of flavor profiles, but limes and oranges can be a good source for a natural acid, too, and ones to consider if the ingredients and produce seem more suited to them as partners.

Before you start adding these fruits, though, do take a look at your recipe and decide how necessary they are. Your wine may not need these additions if the recipe includes citrus, tea, raisins, or other fruits. Anything you do add has the potential – likelihood, even – of changing the flavor of your wine (although if well balanced, it's often for the better, creating a richer, more complex flavor). Use your judgment. I've never found yeast nutrient to be my trouble (but who knows – maybe my wines could have been even better?). If I did feel the need to hedge my bets, Connelly's tea nutrient brew sounds like a pretty safe and natural way to go without adding a lot of chemically-balanced concoctions, and all while keeping it clean, cheap, easy, and simple.

On that note, how much should you use? Following is a basic guide for adding these natural chemical alternatives:

- **Tea:** One cup of strong brewed black tea, or one teaspoon of tea leaves per gallon of liquid
- **Lemon juice or citrus:** One-half a lemon or the juice of one-half lemon per gallon per batch – about equal to one tablespoon of lemon juice (also acceptable – but may commercial lemon juice may contain preservatives)
- **Raisins:** Amounts vary, but a good measure would be ¼ cup raisins per gallon per batch (rinse raisins in hot water, then cold, and cut or chop before adding)

Add these ingredients to the fruit in the primary fermentation stage.

CAMPDEN TABLETS

Campden tablets are the other troubleshooting-type intervention that you may feel a need to resort to at some point. They are also one of the most frequently used chemicals in home winemaking.

Campden tablets are potassium metabisulfite, which is also available in powder form (they are the same additive with the same purpose). Campden tablets are simply a pre-measured, easier-use version of potassium metabisulfite powder, so when we talk about either, the terms are used interchangeably and are the same thing. Most home winemakers use the tablets over the powder, and you hear the tablets talked about more frequently just because of that ease-of-use factor.

Campden tablets are used as a fruit sanitizer prior to making the wine, and also at racking and bottling stages to prevent yeast from becoming active and restarting fermentation. Many people think Campden tablets can be used to stop a fermentation (such as if they want a wine that is less dry or more sweet), but they do not really have the ability to do this. In fact, the experts warn not to try to use Campden tablets this way because it does not work. What Campden tablets can do is create an environment in which minimally active yeast at the end of a fermentation cannot reproduce and therefore cannot restart fermentation. For this reason, they are recommended when back-sweetening wine with a sugar syrup. Adding sugar to sweeten a wine to your taste provides a potential new food source for those sugar-eating yeast. If the yeast is strong enough, even a low level of active yeast (which is not uncommon or even unexpected) can use the newly-introduced sugars as a food source and begin to ferment again. If you are not back-sweetening, however, there isn't likely to be enough of a food source left in a batch to restart fermentation anyway.

The other reason for adding Campden tablets is to help protect the wine from the effects of oxidation—oxygen infiltration over time which can begin to turn wine into vinegar and which can result in blunted, browned colors (which in and of itself does not ruin the wine, just the color of it). In this way, Campden tablets act as preservatives and this is why it is said to help wine keep better for longer periods of time (many years as opposed to one or two).

Now, none of these purposes sound like bad things to avoid in your wine, so why not just use the tablets as the problem preventers they are said to be?

For starters, while Campden tablets are not overly concerning, they are an additive. The most natural wine doesn't use them, and your wine is cheaper and easier for it. There is another very good reason to avoid using Campden tablets, and that is sulfite sensitivity. Sensitivities to sulfites are among the biggest problems people have with drinking wines. Even some commercial producers have turned toward delivering some wines without added sulfites in the interest of serving the sulfite-free population. Added sulfites can produce irritation of the lungs and airways, strong headaches (even while drinking a glass) and more. Now, it does need to be said that *all* wines contain some naturally-occurring sulfites as byproducts of the fermentation process, but at very low natural levels; around ten parts per million as opposed to the fifty to seventy or more parts that you get when using Campden tablets as directed. When people talk about "sulfite-free" wines, they really mean wines with no "added" sulfites, which are the wines that are typically intolerable for affected people.

It is well worth mentioning, too, that it is very easy to get around adding sulfites and using Campden tablets. You simply need to let the process run its course (which it is going to do anyway) and then handle your wine in a way so as to naturally preserve and protect from it oxidation. This is easy to do and not unlike how you should be preparing and handling your wine regardless of additives. Following are some ways that you can produce the same results without having to rely on added sulfites and preservatives:

- **Use alternative household products for cleaning and sanitizing.**
- *Fruit can be easily, cheaply, and naturally cleansed using a solution of **vinegar** and water. Use cool water about the same temperature of the fruit (room temperature for all is best). Add one part vinegar to three parts water (for example, for a gallon of cleaning mix use one quart vinegar and three quarts water). Vinegar is a known natural food and food-safe disinfectant capable of sterilizing a range of organisms from fungi to bacteria. Alcohol levels and carbon dioxide production also have a protective effect in the wine and will also kill off pathogens as the levels rise.*

- *Bleach in water can be used as a sterilizing agent for equipment. This is a very common practice in food processing and production facilities. Chlorine dissipates in contact with air, so after submerging in the bleach and water solution, simply allow to air dry and you will not need to worry about chlorine in your wine. You just need to plan ahead for drying time, but that is really no different than for tablets or other cleansers. Use one tablespoon chlorine bleach per gallon of water. Do not use bleach with added fragrances, cleansers, or thickening agents (such as no- or low-splash bleach) as those are not considered food safe. Regular, cheap, plain old household bleach is all you need and what you should use.*
- **Keep headspaces to a minimum when racking and bottling.** No wine can be stored without any contact with air at all, but you can minimize exposure and prevent potentially problematic oxidation. Fill containers and bottles up to the neck, leaving just a small amount of space between the estimated cork or cap level, and then seal bottles and carboys well.
- **Store racked and bottled wine in a cool area with little light pollution.** Cool and dark will help to keep oxidative effects at bay. It's why wine cellars were created. Recreate the right storage environment as closely as possible.
- **Refrigerate bottled wines.** You are not likely to be able to achieve temperatures as low as what your refrigerator can accomplish, but if you can store some or much of your wine in a low refrigerator (*not* freezing!) you can achieve the same results that sulfites do in terms of oxidation protection. Even back-sweetened wines will not ferment at temperatures in the safe refrigeration range because they are too cold for residual yeasts to be active (37-43^{0}F, the normal food-safe temperatures in the typical refrigerator). Granted this is more difficult, but it is a good option to employ, and even wines you prefer to drink at higher temperatures can simply be brought out ahead of time to enjoy at closer to room temperature.
- **Complete fermentation.** Let the process run its course entirely (complete secondary fermentation) before adjusting. If you do

feel the need to adjust a wine, such as by mixing it with a less-dry wine or making it sweeter by back-sweetening, if the fermentation process has run its course through, those adjustments should not cause an issue. Even with additions and adjustments the alcohol level and remaining active yeast should be at such levels that they cannot support active yeast growth and fermentation. Combined with a good, cool storage arrangement, the odds of natural protection without chemical or additive help are in your favor.

As we've said so many times, the process of making wine in its most simple and natural form doesn't require a lot of interference from us. Nature is quite capable of producing a wonderful wine that can keep well for many months and possibly years to come – by which time you're likely to be into another season of winemaking anyway. These additives are just a couple worth knowing, and these alternatives are quite good at providing natural solutions. As always, this is just more good information for you to have as an option to relax the "rules," give you some great, easy options and to pick and choose your way through cheap, easy, and delicious home winemaking that suits *your* priorities.

CHEMISTRY SET FUN

More technical winemakers use a number of measurements and tools to balance their wine to where they want it to be and to where it fits the "right" levels and balances as proscribed by the wine-making powers that be. If you like science and are willing to spend more on equipment, and more time testing and playing with chemistries, you may want to investigate the more scientific side of the process. Myself, I'm willing to let the natural process play out and make my adjustments by taste and feel (though I rarely, if ever, make adjustments). It's perfectly okay to make this your process, too.

There are a couple of tools that might be of interest and assistance to those in the middle ground. Those are tools for measuring pH/acidity and "specific gravity."

Total Acidity (TA) and pH are related but are not actually the same measure. Both tell the tale of the acidity in the wine, which speaks largely to its flavor. Wine generally falls in the range of 3.0 to 4.0 (some say as high as 4.5) pH. The closer to the 3.0 end, the crisper and more tart the wine will taste. You see this in crisp white wines, typically, while "bigger" red wines are closer to 3.8-4.0. If testing and balancing your wine is of importance or interest to you, you will definitely want to explore the matter further to learn how to qualify your results and how to adjust a wine. There are a number of additives used in these types of adjustments and the adjustments are not always linear depending on what reading you are taking. If you are interested in just some threshold testing, an acidity level reading might help you get to "know" your wines even if you don't intend to go to great lengths of chemical adjustment. For example, if you take your wine's pH it could eventually give you insight into the levels you like and the goals you might want to achieve in your future wines. It is important to note, though, that as with everything in life wine pH does not tell the whole tale – even when adjusting for elements such as acidity, there is much more that plays into the end balance and flavor, including things like tannins, alcohol content, sweetness, and more.

"Specific Gravity" is a different type of measure and probably the one that is the easiest and maybe the most useful to a basic, beginner wine-maker. This is a measure of the sugar content of the must and/or the wine and when you know it, it can tell you things about both sweet-ness and the percentage of alcohol in the wine. It's a pretty simple measure taken with a pretty simple thermometer-like floating device called a hydrometer. Probably the most interesting thing it can tell you is how high an alcohol level your finished wine has. But having the measure can also help you decipher and solve problems during the process, such as determining and treating for a stuck fermentation. The trick of it is, though, that you have to take your first measurements *before* starting the wine (and possibly during, depending on your purpose), and after the wine has finished. If you don't have the initial reading to begin with, you have no point of reference and so later measurements will be meaningless. This is something to keep in mind because if you are interested in knowing the percent alcohol of your wine you'll need to prepare ahead of time or wait until a future batch.

In addition, if you know the sugar content of the must before you start, you can use it to predict the percentage of alcohol that the wine is likely to finish with; not to an exact science or number, because there are always other factors at play, but to a pretty good range of percentage. The potential alcohol that the yeast can produce is relative to the sugar level in the must – because the sugars are, as we now know, the fuel source for the yeast. Therefore, if you are targeting a specific percentage, and you know how much sugar is in the must, you can adjust the amount of sugar that you add to the must for a total level of sweetness and hence a total potential level of alcohol. This is helpful if you are concerned with such things, but even the wine experts agree that it is something of a negotiable point, because a sound recipe will usually put you in optimal ranges anyway and is enough to rely on.

Specific gravity may also be the most meaningful measure in terms of wine "safety" and the reason for that is that alcohol is a preservative and you'll know that as long as you've reached that level of safe alcohol content (targeted around 7 to 8% for a wine to keep well over time) you don't have to worry too much about things that will actually *harm* you. That isn't to say that alcohol level alone ensures that the wine will taste *good*, just that it's not likely to make you sick* (pathogenically speaking...bellyaches and hangovers are yours to own).

Investing in and using tools and measurements such as these is only useful if you plan to put the time into more deliberately designed wines requiring more additive intervention and balancing. It can be a lot for a beginner to take on. What's more, the proof is in the pudding and any more country-style, homestead-type winemaker will tell you that it is more than possible to make a great wine without all the fuss and complication. It's even probable. But if science and titration are your thing, these are a couple of good places to start.

SETTING REALISTIC EXPECTATIONS

So how necessary is it all? All the testing, the balancing, the adding and subtracting, the additional chemicals and additives. Just how important is it?

The answer is really very simple. It's as important as you want it to be. If the minutiae don't matter to you and all you are interested in is making a good, basic, enjoyable wine, if you don't want to be bothered with the many, many options and calculations that make your head spin, if you're happy to take on a tried-and-true method to make some delicious homemade wines, then pay them no importance. Follow the basics and get to it. If what you want is a more balanced, nuanced, tailored wine and you're happy to invest the time and the money, then exploring more of these scientific approaches — and a lot of trial and error – is what will get you there.

The point is, as we've said here, as winemakers and hobbyists and commenters have said, if you enjoy the process and enjoy your product *that* is the point. And it's all you need. Be realistic in your expectations. Play and grow and see the ways that fruits and berries transform when they become wine. Taste other similar styles of wines, like wild wines and country wines, and see what you might reasonably expect to begin with (often you'll find that flavors are much more muted and different than you'd expect anyway – I once drank a tomato wine that tasted *nothing* of tomatoes!). I do suspect Mr. Petersohn, again, said it best:

"I don't try to copy a certain beverage and pretend it tastes just like Pinot Noir or Chateau Briand. My aim is an interesting beverage that can be preserved without refrigeration until it's been consumed. Every bucket, even from the same berry bush, tastes a little different, which keeps things interesting."
- Frank Petersohn

5

THE PROCESS

Are you thinking by now, "Thank goodness!"; "On with it!"; "FINALLY, how to actually *do it!*"?

Fair enough, I don't blame you (and for those of you rebels who just skipped all my hard writing labors, you're forgiven). I like to offer up a solid foundation that I hope answers some of the more common questions and sets the stage well for success, but if all you ever did was follow the instructions and recipes, that should be enough to get you there. And no, that doesn't mean you've just wasted all of that life if you've actually been reading this far; what you've just experienced is the research and learning curve and a bit of the decision-making process I've put myself through over almost a decade of making simple homemade wine. It's the bits and pieces I've looked up and added, or at least considered, as I've learned and grown. I like to offer it as a basis of knowledge and interest and as an example of how you can tweak your own practice to something informed and useful, but still manageably your own.

The process is straightforward and surprisingly simple, especially if you've ever investigated the more complex methods of making wine.

STEP 1: PREPPING FOR THE PROCESS

As with anything, the process starts with the preparation. We've touched on a lot of this in previous discussions about equipment. That is, in fact, the first step of the process: Gathering your equipment and supplies. Note that at this point you won't need all of the equipment and supplies we talked about; some of them will not come into play for a week or more. What you really need on the day you start making your wine are the following pieces of equipment:

- Strainers or colanders for cleaning fruit
- 5-gallon bucket
- Mashing equipment
- Gloves if using
- Large stock pot for dissolving sugar in water
- Miscellaneous kitchen equipment (spoons, bowls, etc.)

Start Clean

Each new stage of the process begins with good cleanliness and wine-making hygiene. As the process goes in stages separated by weeks and even months, there's not a lot of value in cleaning every last piece of equipment until it's time to use it. *Gathering* all of the equipment prior to beginning is a wise step so that you can move right along through each stage without worrying about something not being available or not arriving on time, but in terms of cleaning and sterilizing the individual pieces, that's best done as part of the process at each step.

Cleaning How-to

Cleaning for wine-making equipment is not complex. It's enough to make sure you've brushed and washed away any foreign matter and taken your equipment through a sterilizing rinse.

For washing, a simple hand-wash dish soap is sufficient. Do make sure to rinse the equipment thoroughly to remove all residual soaps. A triple rinse with hot running water should do the trick.

Sterilization is an even simpler process.

1. First, fill a large sink or basin with hot water and your selected sterilizing agent. If you can at least dip each portion of your buckets and jugs and roll or rinse it so that the solution washes over all wine contact surfaces, your basin is big enough.
2. After submerging and rinsing the piece, turn it upside-down onto a rack (preferably, for airflow) or clean surface and allow it to air dry. There is no need to hand-dry the equipment; it will maintain its cleanliness and sterility better if air-dried and the solution can dissipate as it kills pathogens without potentially introducing more from cloths, etc.

In terms of sterilizing solutions for equipment, there are two good options – as discussed in the previous chapter, either chlorine bleach solution or Campden Tablets (potassium metabisulfite). Following is a quick recap on how to sterilize wine-making equipment using either of these two options.

My preferred option is simple household chlorine bleach. Nothing fancy, nothing scented, nothing expensive, just regular-strength normal household bleach. Avoid no- or low-splash versions because they often contain thickening agents that can hang around and aren't strictly considered food safe (whereas a normal chlorine bleach solution at correct concentrations is even accepted for sterilization in licensed kitchens and food establishments).

If using bleach, for every gallon of water, add one tablespoon of bleach.

Campden tablets or potassium metabisulfite sulfite solution is the other option, and the one you'll hear about from wine-making experts. There's nothing "wrong" with it, but it's an added step in ordering and obtaining, a bit more difficult to locate, and a little more expensive (plus, most of us already have bleach at home; simple. Easy.)

If using Campden tablets, crush sixteen tablets for every gallon of water. Dissolve thoroughly in the water before submerging equipment.

It is often said to add citric acid to the mix as well; add ½ teaspoon for every gallon of solution.

STEP 2: GATHER AND PREP YOUR INGREDIENTS

Gathering and sanitizing your equipment is all well and good, but when you start gathering and prepping actual *wine ingredients*, that's when you can really feel like you're getting somewhere.

This is the point where Frank Petersohn would say, *"Find 15-20 pounds of something resembling fruit or vegetables."*

If you're following a specific recipe, you're apt to have a bit more specific measurement than that, but honestly, following his advice works, too, especially if you aren't very particular about producing an exact replica of a wine. Given the differences in fruits and produce from year to year, you're always going to have some variation anyway. And for those times when you find yourself with an abundance of something new that you want to play and experiment with, just the basics will be enough to get you something very good.

Elderberries prepped for must for primary fermentation.

Once you have your grapes or produce, it's time to prep them by first cleaning them, and then de-stemming and de-seeding them to the extent possible. To wash your fruit or produce, go back to one of those options we discussed in the last chapter. Campden tablets are one choice but when used as a produce sterilizer they actually go into the must: Crush one tablet, dissolve in water and then add it to the must, which then MUST sit for 24 hours before continuing and pitching the yeast (otherwise the "good" yeast will die, too). Use Campden tablets or powdered sulfites as directed.

The other option for cleaning produce is to soak your produce in a vinegar and water solution for 20 minutes or more while you get ready for the next step, and then drain and let the produce sit as you de-stem and de-seed. The vinegar will dissipate in the air while you work and there is no waiting period before you can move on...after draining there will not be enough diluted vinegar left to affect anything and the time it takes to prep the fruit will be more than enough to get rid of any light vinegar essence. (Again, the dilution rate for cleaning food with vinegar is one part vinegar to three parts water.)

After you've cleaned your produce you want to get rid of as many stems, pits, and seeds as possible. Some stems, pits, and seeds carry toxic compounds and they can also potentially throw less-desirable flavors, and so you want to get rid of stems and seeds when you can. Here's the thing, though: The extent to which it is possible will depend on what you are making your wine out of and how reasonable it is to be able to remove stems and seeds. Sometimes you are actually better off not trying to go overboard removing seeds because the only viable options cause too much loss and/or break open the seed. It is when seeds are broken open that toxins may become an issue. Intact smaller seeds aren't really a problem, so in things like seeded grapes and berries with small seeds, we leave them and ignore them and just remove as much stem as possible. Do note, though, that this is just why anything sharp or destructive isn't a good idea for making your mash if the seeds cannot be removed. For example, for seeded or pitted large fruits, running the prepped fruit through a food processor or blender is a pretty easy way to mush the fruit for the must. This isn't a good idea for grapes, though, since blending the grapes would cause a lot of nicking and cutting open of the seeds, and those seeds are large enough to make a difference. Tiny seeds like strawberries are less of an issue but I generally find it's not worth the risk or the hassle of machine-blending because they're easy enough to crush by hand as you go.

Following are tips and tricks for preparing some of the more common fruits, berries, and produce. Although not every possibility is listed, you can use this list as a guide for handling other fruits and vegetables.

• Grapes: Remove from stems; do not de-seed but also do not

use any appliance with sharp blades to crush them so that seeds remain intact.

- Berries (i.e. raspberries, blackberries, strawberries, blueberries…): Remove from stems without de-seeding; hand-crush preferable.
- Elderberries: Do not attempt to de-seed but *do* destem as much as possible; stems carry toxins and although some people, especially old-timers, say they throw in bunches stems and all, it is not recommended (besides reasons of toxicity, it will throw off your ingredient measurements by a lot...but safety and toxicity are the primary concern). Fresh, ripe berries come off easily if rolled gently between the fingers or you can use the tried-and-true method of raking the berries off the stems with a fork. You're likely still to get a few stray twigs; pick out as much as possible but don't worry about a few here and there. Elderberries begin to break down quickly after harvest, so plan to work them within about a day and keep them comfortable and cool beforehand.
- Cherries and chokecherries: Remove both pits and stems.
- Apples and pears: Remove stems and seeds; mechanical processing with a food processor or blender is okay after destemming and deseeding (add a small amount of water to blenders to prevent burning out the motor) or simply cut into smaller pieces (you do not need to cut these as small as diced – eighths or sixteenths will suffice.
- Stone fruits (i.e. peaches, plums, apricots): Remove stems, cut open and remove pits, then cut into smaller pieces (quarters or eights) or process in a blender or processor.

If you are using fruit not listed here, simply compare it to the closest relative type and treat similarly.

Step 3: Making the Must and Starting Your Wine

Here is where the fun begins, and the fruit starts to make you believe you might actually make wine.

Once you have removed the stems and seeds as possible, you will need to crush and break up the fruit or berries. What you are going for here is a messy, juicy mix of fruit and juice that exposes a lot of interior and surface area of the fruit. As the fruit ferments, it breaks down and softens and more juice will release but you need to give it the best start that it can have because that won't really amount to a lot in the grand scheme of things. Most especially for things like grapes and berries, you need to "break open" the coats so that that process can really take hold and juices can escape.

For crushing your fruit, you have a few options. The cheapest option is your own two (clean!) hands. Some grapes, fruits, and berries can be irritating to the skin, though, especially when you are working in such large quantities; they can also stain your skin in some very unattractive colors (dark berries in particular), so if you are using your hands you'll want to think hard about wearing a pair of gloves. I find that a lot of times just getting my hands in the pile and squishing away is the easiest way, especially if you are working with very small and soft berries.

Your next cheapest option will be a kitchen or potato masher. This works well for larger berries and grapes. You should work in smaller batches in a bowl so that you make sure you get most of the grapes or berries – missing a few here and there is no big deal and seems to always happen, but you'll want to make sure you break most of them open. With berries and grapes (and technically a grape is a berry), I often end up using a combi-

The making of the musts.

nation of crushing with a hand masher and getting my (gloved) hands juicy.

A household blender or food processor is helpful for mashing fruits batch by batch for those fruits that do not contain seeds that would negatively affect the outcome. Most berries are okay to go through a blender or processor, but you should stay away from it for elderberries or seeded grapes. Given that you have to work in such small batches and most small berries and fruits are easy to crush by hand, you're likely to find it's simply easier to crush and mash using your hands. If you do choose to use a blender do be sure to use a small amount of water in your blender to avoid burning out the motor. In terms of the "cheap" factor, blender and food processors aren't tremendously expensive and are worth mentioning because most of us already own one, but if you are looking at investing in one solely for the purpose of making wine, it's not where I would put my money.

A fruit crusher or fruit press, such as an apple crusher or press used for making apple cider, is an excellent option for crushing and processing fruit and juice if you happen to have access to one. Being something of modern "homesteaders," we did opt to invest in one several years into our wine-making adventures. They do an excellent job preparing any type of fruit for making wine. The trouble is that they do not fall into the category of cheap at all, and you are looking at an investment of probably $300 at minimum for a full setup. Their uses go beyond wine-making musts,

Though expensive, if a fruit press is available it is a very handy wine-making tool to have!

though (there's always that apple cider thing!), so if you plan to make large quantities of wine regularly and maybe have an interest in cider, it's an investment worth considering.

Another option is to consider purchasing only the fruit crusher to get you started (which is sold separately from the press and is cheaper), which will still take a lot of the labor out of the process for you while really breaking up your produce to release juice and expose surface area. One other note: Fruit presses work great even on the smallest of berries (it's been an elderberry lifesaver for me). You'll want to make sure that you purchase a fine-mesh pressing bag or two to go with it so that you don't lose small berries out of the sides. Always reserve the pressings even when bags are used, as you'll want to add them back into the juice and must – they still have a lot to give to the wine and nuanced flavors to impart that make your wine better than just fermented juice. If staining the bag is not a concern for you, you can also use it as a fermenting bag, which saves a straining step later on.

STEP 4: PRIMARY FERMENTATION

Now we pull our ingredients together to build the base of the wine and begin the fermentation process. Fermentation is a multi-step process that takes place over several weeks, in a couple of stages. This first stage is called "primary fermentation."

Take your clean, food-safe five-gallon bucket. Dump all of your must into the bucket, juice, pulp, and all.

Now you need to dissolve your sugar in a quantity of water. Ten pounds of sugar is the basic measurement for this step. Yes, ten pounds sounds like a lot of sugar, but that yeast is hungry and no, it doesn't mean you end up with a sugar-syrup of a wine! Put the sugar in a large stock pot and add enough water to cover the sugar with about an inch or two over it. If this does not seem to be enough water to dissolve the sugar, add a little more but be careful not to use too much water – when you add this dissolved sugar/water mixture to the must, you want to be able to add it all in so that you don't lose the sugar/yeast feed proportion. You will also need enough headspace in the bucket to accommodate for bubbling and rising of the must. Yes, like bread, the yeast will bubble and raise the ingredients and if you don't leave yourself that headspace, you'll have a pretty ugly bubbled-over mess to clean up. The measurement of water is not exact here and the reason for that is that each fruit, each must, will differ in the amount of juice and volume of must produced, so each batch will have a slightly different amount of room left in the bucket. You may need to eyeball it to estimate how much room you have left for the water/sugar mixture once you have your quantity of juice and must in your bucket.

Dissolve sugar in about half of the water so that you know all of the sugar and water mixture will fit into the primary fermentation bucket. More water can be added as needed later.

In general, try starting with two gallons of water to ten pounds of sugar. Note that if you need to adjust something for the sake of volume and available space, adjust the *water*, not the sugar – that sugar quantity should not be changed unless a recipe that calls for a different amount. In any case, it is important to use all of the sugar the recipe calls for. Stir the sugar and water and heat on the stovetop, bringing it to a simmer, until all the sugar is dissolved in the water. Stir frequently so that the sugar does not burn on the bottom before it dissolves into the water. When there is no sugar left in the bottom of the pot and you have a clear-ish liquid, remove it from the heat and let it cool until you are ready for it. It's a good idea to do this before you start mashing your fruit. This will give the too-hot sugar syrup time to cool off so that it won't kill the yeast when it is added.

After you have heated and dissolved the sugar into the water, remove from heat and let the mixture cool. When your must of mashed fruit and juice is ready, combine the must and the cooled sugar-water together in your 5-gallon bucket and give it a stir through. The most important thing in this step is NOT to add the yeast (or "pitch" as it is so called) when the must temperature is too high; yeast begins to die at temperatures over 120 °F, so anything pushing that or over that is going to start compromising your yeast's ability to thrive, multiply, and sustain fermentation. Strangely enough, very clear direction on what temperature to pitch wine yeast at isn't that easy to find; what is out there relies a lot upon the specific wine "kit" you buy. And like many other aspects of making wine according to the experts, there are lots of opinions and lots of picky variations depending on the fruit, the goal, the style...the list goes on and on.

The older timers didn't worry that much over the perfect temperature for this or that down to the degree. They worked in ranges and comfort zones, often dictated by choosing the right location (as we talked about earlier in the yeast chapter). Their directions say things more like, "warm" and honestly, though I do think using a decent kitchen thermometer helps ensure good results, I've made plenty of wine without being picky to the degree, and it's worked. Frank's instruction here is, "Take a cup or two of your must, with enough water that it's not too thick, make it nice and warm."

What's "nice and warm"? In the interest of giving some guidance, let's try to assign some numbers. There are two numbers we want to target here. One is the temperature of the must after you have added the dissolved water and sugar to the fruit pulp and juice. Because you have probably simmered the water to a pretty high temp to dissolve all that sugar, the temperature can be too high and can potentially kill the yeast if it's over 120°F. You'll need to let it cool down so that your yeast isn't killed when you pitch it into the must. Ideally the temperature of your must when you add the yeast should be just a little higher than the optimal temperature for fermentation – around 80^0 to 85^0 would be good and it will cool down to its steady fermentation temperature over the next few hours.

The other number we care about is the temperature of the water when you rehydrate the yeast (what Frank calls "nice and warm"). The experts put this at a pretty narrow range of between 100 and 105°F. For this step, when the temperature of your must is about ready for the yeast, take a cup or two of the must and add a bit of water if you need to make it more fluid. Shooting for a temp in that 100-105° range, sprinkle the yeast granules over the top. Let them sit and hydrate for 15 minutes without stirring. After 15 minutes, give the mixture a stir. Let sit for about 15 minutes more, until foamy. Now add this proofed yeast mixture to the bucket of must, and again stir through to distribute more evenly.

And that's it! You've just started your primary fermentation! *You've done the big work of making your home-made wine!* Yes, there's more to do in the future but a lot of the work now is in patiently impatiently waiting.

Now, take that beautiful bucket of will-be wine and place it in your previously identified fermentation location. To help control fruit flies and their ilk, you can cover the bucket with a clean linen kitchen towel, some plastic wrap with several holes poked in it, or the bucket lid just set on top – but not tightened down, or it'll blow

Bubbling should be easily visible during the first week of fermentation (but is often hidden until the cap is stirred and gases are released).

off as gasses build up inside. Once a day for the next week, come back to your brew and stir the mix. This will break up the "cap" (the risen fruit pulp which floats to the top and acts as, well, a cap), which will release gas build-up and give all the pulp a chance at contact and fermentation so that you get the most possible out of your wine.

Keep an eye daily on the activity of your wine must. After about 24-48 hours, you should be seeing some quite vigorous activity and bubbling. This will keep up for about the next week, tapering off towards the end of the seven-day period. When the activity starts to slow – near the end of the week, give or take a day or two – it's time to move on to the next step of the wine-making process.

STEP 5: STRAINING AND SECONDARY FERMENTATION

After that first week the fast and furious work of primary fermentation is over, and you will notice that the vigorous bubbling of those early to mid-week days have slowed. They should not have stopped completely, but you will begin to see a noticeable change. The fermentation process, however, is not over; not even close. Your wine will need about another four weeks for fermentation to complete.

"When the ugly bubbling has slowed down, use sieves, colanders, or rags to strain the ugly mess." -Frank Petersohn

The goal in this step is two-fold: First, to remove as much of the pulp and bulk waste from the will-be wine and second, to "rack" it into a long-term fermentation vessel.

The first part of this step is fairly simple but does take a bit of time and can be messy, so you'll want to prepare yourself and not try to crunch this into a window where you only have a few minutes. Leave yourself at least an hour for the active work. It's better if you can do this on a day when you will be around for a block of a few hours, just for additional hanging time and time for cleanup.

Pro tip: Lay some waste newspaper down in a sizable area where you will strain to catch drips and splashes. When the weather is nice, I've even opted to do this outside on a porch.

When you get into this process you'll find pretty quickly that you have a layer of large, pulpy chunks of

mashed fruit, skins, and seeds, that are pretty easy to bail out and then you also have a layer of fine particles suspended in and laying on the bottom of the fermenting wine juice. For this step, your main goal is to get the biggest of the chunks out. It's also good to get as much of the fine sediment out as possible, but do not be concerned when you can't get all of that out at this point – much of it will remain suspended in the juice; much

Strain and discard solid skins, pulp, and seeds and reserve liquid for secondary fermentation.

of it will strain out if you use permeable cloths or fine mesh; a good amount of it will remain but will settle out along with even more fine "lees" in the next step of the process and will be dealt with later. If you come out of this step with a murky dark liquid, you're still doing it right and you've got nothing to worry about.

For equipment here you'll want to gather the best straining pieces you have. As discussed in chapter one, this may be dedicated equipment you have invested in, or it may be kitchen equipment – strainers and colanders and the like – that you are pressing into use. Either gets the job done. I tend to use some combination of both. You will also want to gather two additional pieces of your large equipment and of course, clean it prior to use. Get one of your clean five-gallon food-safe pails. You may even want two, to make it easier to work in batches and stages. You will also need your four- or five-gallon "carboy" (real carboy if you've invested, large plastic water jug if you've gone the cheap and lighter route). At the end of this step you will also need whatever you are using as your "airlock." Again, this can either be the real deal or the pieces to make up your cheap and easy homemade version, which will work just as well.

Everyone seems to have their own little method for how to best strain the pulp from the juice. I use a two-step process where I strain with a larger-holed colander set over an extra bucket and/or use a handled mesh strainer to bail out the bulk of the large pulp first. Then I use my fine-mesh strainer and pour that quick-strained juice into a second clean pail. For this I use one of our fine-mesh honey strainers designed to sit in the top of a five-gallon pail, or a stainless-steel colander lined with clean linen "flour sack" towels...towels I'm happy to stain, because they will! Mr. Petersohn's suggestion was to strain through nylon panty hose with the leg cut off (new and clean, of course, and the larger the size the better). After you've strained the pulp, if you have a safe place to hang the pulp-filled nylon above the bucket to drain for a few hours then you can recover a fair amount of trapped liquid, reduce waste, and loss of volume – because your wine is precious, and although you can't save it all, you'll want to save as much as possible! Incidentally, if you do have a fruit press, you can also bail the pulp out into a fine pressing bag and then press it, spout over your bucket, to reclaim your juices. It's a great way to maximize your yield if you have the equipment available to you (but not a necessary investment for the hundreds of dollars that you'll spend on the press).

**It's worth mentioning here, that another option is to use a fermenta-
tion bag – either a homemade variety or one purchased – during your
first fermentation. This is much like the bag that you would use if you
were pressing fruit with a fruit press. In fact, a fruit press bag would
work. Many of the bags sold as fermentation bags are the same as the
pressing bags; you'll often see them sold as multipurpose bags for
pressing, fermenting, or straining. Fermentation bags are large bags
that roughly fit a five-gallon bucket. Depending on where you source
them, they run somewhere in the range of $12 to $20 (do shop around
a bit; there's not a lot of difference in design or construction, but there
is an appreciable price difference). To use a fermentation bag, simply
put it onto your bucket and put the pulp *inside* the bag. At this point,
you can choose to cinch it up or not, but if you leave it open then you
can still stir and break up the "cap" as your first week's fermentation
goes on. Just keep an eye to make sure that the bag or its drawstring
are not acting as a wick and wicking baby wine out onto your floor!

Where a fermentation bag is most helpful is when it comes time to
strain the pulp from the first fermentation – no messy dumping and
straining. Simply lift the bag out and let it hang over the bucket for a
while to drain. You may or may not find that the resulting wine is
murkier, but it will certainly get out the largest pulp in one easy step,
leaving you with a young wine ready to rack for secondary
fermentation.

However, if you choose to do it after you have strained out all the pulp
and let it "hang" to drain the reserves, it's time to set your wine up for
the long fermentation period, the secondary fermentation. This stage
will take about a month and by the end of it, you will have a very
young wine and the fermentation stage will be complete, but the wine
will want for some aging. This step simply consists of getting your
juice into an air-tight jug for a protected long fermentation period.
What is often referred to as "secondary fermentation" and/or
"racking."

You'll likely want a funnel, the largest mouth you have whose bottom
sits well inside the mouth of your jug. Pour your strained fermented
juice into the water jug or carboy. Now top the wine with enough cool

to luke-warm water to nearly fill the jug. Aim to fill close to the neck so that you reduce any potential airspace and spoilage. This is more important in future rackings because at this point the wine is still fermenting, and so it will have some protection from the carbon dioxide blanket that is formed over the top of the fermenting wine by the fermentation process. Still, it's good to reduce potential air contamination as much as possible. If your wine is not going to be bumped and moved during the secondary fermentation process – and you should avoid this as much as possible – then you can feel pretty safe about leaving a little extra room if you need to, even if your wine volume does not reach the top of the jug. Again, there are differing opinions here, but that is the natural process and protection of it. I prefer to safeguard myself a little and take up that airspace just in case the jug gets jostled and the fermentation has stopped before I'd expected, so that there is still not a risk of air spoilage.

The amount of water you add at this point is less of a science. Frank said simply (and this is the advice in most recipes), "add enough water to almost fill" the container. In general, this instruction is correct – add enough cool to luke-warm water to fill the jug up to the base of the neck. However, if you've had a low juice yield, it's possible to water the wine down too much and result in a weak wine. So, while my instruction also would be to fill the jug close to the bottom of the neck, if you think this is starting to get too watery, you can stop short. Kind of eyeball the wine and try not to let it get too thin (recognizing that it may take a few times making wine before you really get a feel for this). Don't be too scared of adding too much or too little water – you won't ruin your wine; it will just be different. We're talking about the difference between a lighter or heavier wine and/or one that might turn out less flavorful than you'd like, and a lot of that comes down to preference and taste anyway. Usually when I make wine, we're talking about adding another ten to twenty percent volume of water. So, if you have about 4 gallons in the jug, add up to another gallon of water going into the second fermentation but if the juice is looking light, do something more like ½ to ¾ gallon.

Part of the idea here is that you are trying to get the volume up in the carboy or jug to reduce airspace (headspace) and contact surface area for the secondary fermentation to prevent spoilage. Now, this isn't as important in the secondary fermentation stage as it is during later rackings. This is because your wine is still fermenting. It's still producing that heavy carbon dioxide that will lay over the top of the wine and protect it because the oxygen cannot get through the carbon dioxide. The risk is that if the vessel gets jostled you could potentially introduce some air. But this is also why we fashion some sort of "air-lock." So really, if your wine is kept safe and undisturbed with a decent airlock (whether homemade or purchased), even if you must leave a volume of open space in the jug, all should be okay. In later stages the headspace/airspace/contact surface issue is a potential problem, but there are steps to take to address this without compromising your wine (which we will talk about in the next section on racking). If you are concerned about it, these are steps you could incorporate now, but they are unnecessary as long as fermentation is continuing and providing that protective carbon dioxide layer, further protected by the airlock you will install.

This, of course, brings us to the airlock. As mentioned, you can certainly purchase an airlock, but you can also easily fashion one that will do the trick just fine. What's most important here is not the *kind* of airlock you choose to use – commercial or home-fashioned – what's important is that you *have one* and that it is *airtight*.

The purpose of the airlock is to let built-up air and carbon dioxide gas *out* of the fermentation vessel or carboy while *not* allowing air and oxygen *in*. This is done by providing a sort of ventilation tube in combination with a protective portion of water. In a commercial airlock the water goes into the bottom "u" of the tube and settles there for the duration. Kind of like a u-shaped trap in a sink drain. In the home-made version, the water is just water in a jar that the tube feeds into. Either is fine, so the choice is yours. Just be sure that if you do decide to buy an airlock that it fits the mouth of your jug tightly. If there's question, fall back on your stand-by duct tape and seal it up around the mouth.

To make a homemade airlock, you'll need just a few supplies:

- The cap that came on the water jug.
- A length of tubing, any small diameter, cut long enough to reach the jar of water (the jar will sit on the floor next to the jug of wine, so keep this in mind for length)
- A roll of duct tape to seal it all together.
- Something for cutting tubing and the cap; a razor knife works well (and of course here I must tell you to use caution and not cut yourself).

Cheap homemade airlocks are simple to make.

To make the airlock, cut a small hole in the center of the cap of the jug. Often water-cooler jug caps have a sort of molded indentation that dips down and you can simply slice off the bottom of the indent. Make the hole big enough for the tube to feed through it, but not so small that the air/gas-flow will be kinked or cut off. Feed the tubing through your hole – just far enough to hold stably, but not so far that it goes too far into the jug neck or down into the jug itself. You do not want the tubing to touch or be submerged in the liquid. You want it to act as something like a chimney for ventilation where first air and then carbon dioxide gas can be pushed up and out and escape. with the tube threaded through, tape it in place with the duct tape.

Now install your airlock onto the fermenting jug of wine and tape it well to seal off any potential air inlets. Make sure to seal well around the tubing as well as around the mouth of the jug and cap. Duct tape is cheap and you can just rip it off when the time comes later, so don't be shy and be sure to seal up any air holes.

Once firmly in place, put a couple of cups of water into a sturdy jar, heavy enough that it won't get tipped over (a quart mason jar works well). Place the free end of the tube into the water. Now, as gases build up in the wine, the heavier carbon dioxide will sit atop the wine's surface as it forces the air in the jug out through the tube, into the water where it can bubble up and out, and the jug will not be sealed tight and build up gas and pressure and cause a messy explosion.

With a little Googling, you can come up with other very cheap and easy homemade airlock solutions, with which people have had varying results but you are free to choose and try them out. One popular method is to take a balloon, poke several holes in it, and then stretch it over the mouth of the fermenting jug. Gasses can inflate the balloon and allow them to escape through the pinholes, but the holes seal up when not under pressure and don't allow air back in. Some people find this to be a super-cheap method with good success; others have issues with breaking balloons and balloons whose holes seem to stick and find themselves with balloons popping off instead of venting air and gas. It is an option.

A bit of tubing and tape with an end in the water and your homemade airlock is complete!

Others have topped their secondary fermenter with layers of plastic wrap and poked holes through the wrap – a similar method to the balloon. Some people even do this using a bucket as their secondary fermentation vessel. If you try it, what you will want to be very sure of is that the plastic wrap stays tightly adhered to the top – consider large rubber bands to hold the plastic wrap in place, or perhaps that tape again (just keep in mind that this is a seal you need to keep for a month and maybe a little more, and having to disturb or replace it is not ideal for your wine). It is a method, though, and it certainly fits our criteria for inexpensive.

The one thing you absolutely *do not* want to do at this point is to seal your container up tightly. This is not the time for a screw top, sealed bucket top, or lid. *Gasses will build up and push out air and carbon dioxide until fermentation stops!* If you don't provide a pressure-relief, your container will create one for you, and the resulting blow will be messy at the very least, possibly even unsafe and dangerous at its worst.

With your airlock fashioned, now it's time to lay your fermenting wine to "rest" (a real misnomer because this is a very active phase); you want to place your unit in that previously-designated area where it can sit undisturbed, untouched, and un-jostled for about the next month, give or take. The temperature should be relatively steady and draft-free, at around 75°F ideally, as previously discussed. This done, all you have to do now is let your wine quietly bubble away as the yeast grows and multiplies, feasts and turns that juicy water into wine.

Keep a check on things now and again over the course of the next month. Look closely to see if the wine is still bubbling (in a "real" airlock, you'll see some slow bubbles; in a jug with a homemade airlock, you can shine a flashlight through the side of the jug and see bubbles, like soda bubbles, moving up). As long as the bubbling continues, the yeast is doing its job. It will slow and eventually stop as the fermentation completes in the late weeks of the month. This is all perfectly fine and there is just not anything else for you to do at this point but let nature take its course. That said, if the bubbling and fermentation should stop for some reason, and it happens to the best of us, you may need to introduce more yeast to get it kick-started again. This happens less frequently than you'd think, though, especially if you've followed basic wine-making instructions. If you *do* think you need to restart a fermentation, take some time to make sure it's really not fermenting. The bubbling is subtle and can be hard to see. It slows as it goes and as food supplies are depleted by the yeast. This is what is supposed to happen. Before you take action and add yeast to it, take two or three days and check the wine daily for signs of bubbling and fermentation before you jump in.

**Tip: When you rack your wine for the secondary fermentation, use a sharpie or dry erase marker and write the type of wine and the date it was racked on the top of the jug. This way you won't forget when you racked the wine, or which wine it is — because as much as we think we'll remember, life likes to get in the way and play tricks on us, and if you end up with more than one wine

stewing it can suddenly get very easy to mix them up. I find this little trick to be a good reminder and a real sanity-saver!

Step 6: Racking and Bottling

Once fermentation is complete following the second stage, it is time to either rack or bottle the wine. The wine should be ready for the next stage in about four weeks. Use your calendar as your guide, but also take some time to look at the wine itself and look for signs of completed fermentation. For our cheap and easy purposes, we will focus on the observable, visual signs of fermentation. If you do work with a hydrometer, there are measurements that can be taken, too, but a little observation is a pretty good way to see when your fermentation is finished. Ideally what you'll see is this:

- **No more bubbles.** Above all, look for the bubbling action to have stopped. You should not see active carbonation bubbles rising to the top (save for a little trapped gas here and there if you jiggle the jug). If your wine looks something like soda in a glass, you can bet your fermentation is not complete. If you did use a commercial airlock, look for slowed or stopped, infrequent and irregular bubbling in the airlock water. Note that some bubbles can occur from temperature and pressure differences in- and outside the jug, so it's not an absolute indicator, but if the bubbling in an airlock stays steady, your wine isn't there just yet. At the end of fermentation, when I think my wine should be finished, I'll give the jug a good jiggle (without disturbing the airlock) and see if it bubbles up, then observe it for a few days to make sure nothing reinvigorates and steady bubbling doesn't start again. If it does, I give things another week and then reassess.
- **Look for clearing wine.** As the yeast dies, it falls to the bottom with other sediments and creates what are called "lees." When this happens, the wine becomes much clearer than you've ever seen it – almost transparent except for the color of the wine. Of course, whiter, lighter wines are easier to tell and the darker

the wine the harder it will be to see through it, but you will notice a real change in the clarity of the wine. Even the darkest wines will become more "shiny" and almost jewel toned. If you've been observing your wine regularly all along (and you should be – it's fun and interesting stuff to watch!), this will become easy for you to see as things progress. It often helps me to shine a little flashlight through the side of the wine to see the clarity. Just note that if you have lifted, jiggled, or disturbed the jug, you may need to let it settle for a few hours or a day before checking the clarity, because moving the jug can shake up the sediment layer in the bottom.

- **Look for lees.** Lees are the sediment layer that falls out to the bottom of the fermenting wine. They are comprised of pieces of pulp and other organics and also of dead yeast. As fermentation completes, these elements fall out and make quite a thick layer (often a solid couple of inches) in the bottom of the fermenter. If you are seeing this thick layer of sediment on the bottom of your fermenter, it's a very good indication that fermentation is at or near completion.

Of course, none of these things alone is enough to decide that your fermentation is complete. Taken in combination, though, along with a little bit of tracking and timing to know when your wine *should* be finished fermenting, they are pretty reliable. Even then there is a slim chance that your wine fermentation may not be all the way complete, but it's unlikely if you have the trifecta of factors of inactivity, clarity, and abundant lees.

A thick layer of sediment on the bottom of your wine, called "lees", is a good sign of completed secondary fermentation.

Understanding why you might be experiencing a stuck fermentation to begin with can also help you decide if it really is stuck fermentation or if your fermentation is complete.

Fermentation that has not completed all the way through is referred to as "stuck." Stuck fermentations happen when something slows the yeast's action to such a degree that it becomes either very slow or dormant and inactive. Depending on the cause, a stuck fermentation can restart if the situation is corrected, either intentionally or accidentally. One of the most common reasons for fermentation to become stuck is temperature – too cool and/or too fluctuating. This may make the wine appear to have completed fermentation because you will not see much bubbling action; maybe none at all. When the wine is shaken up a bit and moved to a warmer location – such as when you are preparing to siphon and rack or bottle your wine – the yeast may become reinvigorated and may "wake up" and begin feeding again. That's good because at least your wine can finish now, but less ideal if you have gone as far as bottling your wine. The risk isn't so much that the wine can't finish fermenting in your bottles; it's more that you will end up with wine with sediment in the bottom (think individual bottles with their own lees and small sediment layer). More importantly, you will have bottles with the potential to build pressure and blow off caps and corks.

SIGNS OF STUCK FERMENTATION

For this reason, it's a good idea to have some idea of what the difference between a stuck or incomplete fermentation and a complete fermentation might be.

- **Seemingly "complete" fermentation in short time.** It really should take your wine a month, and maybe more, to completely ferment and clear. Even five weeks is not abnormal. While the bubbling of your wine will slow by *a lot* as compared to the first weeks, it should not stop in under three weeks in most cases. There are some exceptions – a higher than ideal fermentation temperature chief among them. It is possible for a warm fermentation to make a complete fermentation happen very quickly, but otherwise, if you're at week two or early in week three and there's nothing happening, suspect a stuck fermentation.

- **Wine that still tastes sweet.** The idea is that the sugars in the wine must are the food source for the yeast, and the yeast should keep "eating" until their food is gone. If you taste a little sample of your must and you're tasting something very noticeably sweet (it will register as too sweet on your palate), your fermentation might not be complete.
- **High Hydrometer reading.** If you did use a hydrometer, your specific gravity reading should be 1.000 or lower. Higher than that, you still have available sugars.
- **No bubbling, but no lees, either.** If you don't observe carbonating bubbling action, but you also do not see a significant amount of settled-out sediment in the bottom of your fermenter, it's more likely that the wine is either not finished or that fermentation is slowed and stuck. The amount of lees will vary depending on things like the type of fruit or ingredient, but in general, in a five-gallon batch of wine, you can expect an inch or two or more of settled lees by completion (in my experience an inch has been a minimum).
- **Murky, opaque, and/or cloudy wine.** As mentioned, clarity tells you quite a bit. If your wine is still murky and cloudy, it's probably not finished and if this happens in conjunction with no action (bubbling), then it's probably stuck.
- **Cold fermentation room temperature.** If any of the previously mentioned signs have occurred and you know that the temperature of your fermentation area has not been a pretty steady 70-75 degrees, you can suspect, or at least test, for an incomplete fermentation. Do this first through observation of all those signs in this section and the preceding section, but also do this simple little test: Move your fermenter full of wine to a warmer room, at least 70 degrees...maybe your kitchen or the place where you will be siphoning the wine to rack it. Give it a stir or a shake or a pretty good jostle so that you disturb the lees in the bottom; this will expose any remaining viable yeast cells to favorable conditions if they exist. Keep the airlock in

place and let the wine sit for two or three days. If the warmer wine starts bubbling again, give the wine another week and reassess. If it stays pretty boring, it's time to move on with things.

This little temperature test is always a good idea, even if you are pretty sure your fermentation is complete. It just doesn't hurt to move the wine a couple of days beforehand to the place where you will siphon it – I often do this just for the sake of letting any lees that get disturbed settle to the bottom again. If you think a couple of days ahead and do this before you are actually doing the racking, it allows everything time to calm back down and see if anything changes.

The most important thing to know is that most times, the wine-making process does its own thing. Yeast and nature take their own course. Stuck and incomplete fermentations are the exception, not the norm, and so while it is worth knowing what to keep an eye out for, it's nothing you should let yourself get overly concerned about. If you observe the basic signs of complete fermentation and you know enough time has passed, you can be reasonably assured your fermentation is complete and your wine is ready to move on to the next stage. And one final tip – an extra week on the lees with the airlock in place is not enough to "ruin" your wine. If in doubt and it makes you more comfortable, go ahead and give it a bit more time.

TO RACK OR TO BOTTLE?

With the secondary fermentation complete, it is now time to siphon your new wine off the lees of the secondary fermentation vessel and either rack it a second time or bottle it and cork it for storage.

Which should it be?

There's no straight answer to this question. Whether you rack your wine after fermentation has completed or whether you bottle it is up to you, and everyone makes a little bit of a different choice. There are pros and cons to each.

Why Bottle Right After Secondary/Completed Fermentation

The best argument for bottling right away after the secondary fermentation has completed is convenience. If you bottle right away, you can be done actively dealing with the wine. Hence, if you're pretty confident that your fermentation is completed, you have a cool place for storage, and you want to end the active phase of your wine-making process, go ahead and bottle the wine after the complete secondary fermentation.

Another reason to bottle rather than rack the wine directly after secondary fermentation is if you plan to drink the wine as a young wine, say within the next three months. Yes, wine "rules," say you must age everything to make it good; but really, once fermentation is complete, there is no reason you can't drink your wine right now. It should also be noted that while overall it is safe to say that any wine will benefit from at least a short period of age and rest, many country wines and fruit wines, especially those without added preservatives and sulfites, are best enjoyed towards the younger side of life, say between 18 to 24 months have passed; so that is something to consider for our simpler, less-preserved and chemically-profiled wines. There are some exceptions – darker, heavier wines such as elderberry being one that is said to benefit greatly from a six- to twelve-month aging period. (As a side note, we enjoy more elderberry wine in our home than any other. Perhaps a stray bottle or two makes it as long as six months of age, and the harshness that can come out in elderberry does seem to mellow out with that age, but no one here can tell you whether waiting for a year or more does it any further good!)

Taste, complexity, finish...these are all subjective things that have worked themselves into winemaking as "rules," but which really don't make a difference to safety. The real bottom line is if you like your wine, if you sample it out and think you'll be drinking it soon, if you've made the wine before and have enjoyed it young, bottle it and drink it. If you want to give it some time to see how much better it can be, do that. If you want to split the batch and do something like a half-

and-half racking and bottling, you can do that, too (and we'll talk about how to do that in a moment).

Bottling sooner rather than later can also help prevent some of the oxidation and spoilage that can occur in storage. Something people do not often realize is that corked bottles in storage do continue to "breathe," however minimally. When stored wine experiences changes in storage room conditions (temperature being the biggest culprit), the wine inside the bottles expands and contracts and when that happens, it pulls very minute amounts of air in and out, "breathing in" unde-tectable trace amounts of oxygen. It's an effect that stacks up little by little over time and can impact the quality of the wine (although this would take quite a while and in smaller home batches, you're more likely to go through the wine than to have it around long enough to suffer any appreciable ill-effects). The point is, air intake happens; and when this cumulative effect takes place, it has less of an impact on a smaller portion of bottled wine than it does on a large, racked bulk quantity of wine. The effects are amplified when a large volume is "breathing" as opposed to a relatively small amount in a bottle. Also, as you'll be more likely to start using the bottled wine earlier in its life if it's available to you, you put less of the wine at risk. Even if you lost a few bottles at the very end of your use and run, you won't have spoiled the whole batch. Do keep in mind that this applies more to racking and storing in large quantities for a long period of time – if you are just racking for another month or two, it's less of an issue. Also, good storage can help mitigate the effect, which we'll talk more about later.

Another argument in favor of bottling over racking following the secondary fermentation is that you lose a little of the wine every time you rack it. This is because you can only siphon down to just above the lees, and you can't ever get every bit of liquid without also sucking up the lees – exactly what you are trying to remove from your wine. Now, this is something of an arguable point because you do need to get your wine away from that sediment, so to an extent the loss is a necessary one. Siphoning off the lees the first and second time is absolutely necessary. Whether you rack and plan to siphon a third or subsequent time, at some degree of wine loss, is your decision to make. Some factors to consider when making this choice: Loss of volume means you will have less finished wine, and it also invites the problem of having too much contact surface and headspace in the next racking vessel, something that becomes a bigger issue the older the wine is because oxidation is a bigger risk for the wine as it ages. You will have to have a plan for dealing with the headspace so that you don't ruin your wine in subsequent rackings.

Finally, multiple rackings also expose your wine to oxidation and potentially spoilage organisms as well. Here we are not just talking about oxidation from headspace leftover in the vessel, but the air that the wine will come into contact with while it's open and that may work into the wine through aeration – much like it does with water in a faucet. It's just a fact of life that the more times you handle something, the more times you risk contamination...in this case, contamination in the form of environmental and trapped air and also contamination in the form of environmental pathogens and organisms that may spoil the wine. Truth be told, as alcohol is a preservative, organisms are less likely to be your problem, but it can happen and the more buckets, containers, bottles, hoses, and so on that your wine runs through, the more opportunities it has to pick up something in the equipment. Even the best practices and most sterile environments can't ever guarantee 100%.

Why Rack Right After Secondary/Completed Fermentation

It may sound by now that I am against any further racking after the completed secondary fermentation. That really is not the case. In fact, when I am able to let my patient self prevail, I prefer a third bulk racking for my homemade wines. More often, I end up bottling it because I'm impatient and want to get on with the drinking of it; but really, the happiest medium I've found is to rack off the wine for an extra month, then siphon it off any newly-settled sediment or lees, and then bottle it and start enjoying it while it is still relatively young. I find this to be the best balance for my un-sulfited, untreated wines.

Why do I find this to be the best route? For the very reasons that argue in favor of bulk racking following the secondary fermentation.

First off, if you go directly to bottling from the secondary fermentation you risk having sediment in your bottles of wine. It's not that this ruins the wine, but these are, essentially, very low levels of lees that can affect the taste of the wine; mostly, though, sediment like this just doesn't look very appealing, and while you can usually pour most of the bottle for serving without disturbing the sediment, you'll either be tossing out the bottom of the bottle or getting a very murky last glass or two of your wine. There are a couple of ways to deal with this if it does happen. If you run the wine through some sort of fine filter when you rack it, it can help catch some of that sediment. Filtering cannot, however, catch sediment that is still suspended in the wine that has yet to fall out. You can also take an extra step when you serve the wine – decant the wine through a very fine muslin or butter cloth or filter into a different serving carafe; the drawback here is that if you are just trying to enjoy a glass or two for the evening, you have to decant the whole bottle; and your homemade wine, with all this fabulous flavor and effort, is not something you want to have to waste. And so, a good solution for clearer wine is to take an extra month or so, let a little more sediment settle out, and then bottle the wine for a clearer, better, more enjoyable homemade wine.

Secondly, and perhaps most importantly (at least for your floors and ceilings), racking your wine a second time hedges against an incomplete fermentation and exploding bottles. Ideally, when you rack wine any time after the secondary fermentation you should have a tight lid on the "carboy" (a cap or rubber stopper – you wouldn't usually use an airlock at this point) If you have some concerns over whether there is some residual fermentation, you could install a good airlock system again – just make very sure that you check it for adequate water level weekly, and perhaps even replace the airlock with a full cap or stopper after a week or two when you feel more secure about the fermentation being complete. Myself, I use the tight lid designed for my jugs and then seal them up with duct tape just to be sure I have no air leaking in.

A third racking also gives your wine the opportunity to age as one bulk unit, which contributes to finish and complexity. The fact that the wine is aging as one large bulk unit is said to help it age with a better finish and contributes to a more uniform batch of bottles in the end. There is some argument over this...not really "against" it, but some feel the difference is negligible. One more thing that some do, some don't, and you should decide what you prefer.

Racking for a third or subsequent time also gives you the opportunity to add your own flavor and complexity elements; for example, if you wanted to "oak" the wine with oak chips or in an oak vessel, or if you wanted to back-sweeten the wine for more of a sweet or dessert wine. A later racking would be the time to perform that operation.

Another reason to rack after the second fermentation is to successively get your wine off the lees. Ideally, with fermentation complete, you shouldn't produce much more sediment. However, all wines, all batches, act a little differently and when you *do* have wine with late lees, you don't really want your wine sitting on the lees. (While it is true that there is a process of flavoring wine by aging on the lees ["Sur lie"], it's not something to just wing and you really want to do your research first – it's more involved than simply letting wine sit on the layer indefinitely.) The rule is that after completion you do not want to leave your wine sitting on more than one-half inch of lees, and/or on lees for more than two months. If you plan to age your wine longer prior to bottling, and you have significant lees in the bottom, siphon it off, fill the headspace, and rack it in a new vessel, discarding the sediment. Likewise, if you did "oak" the wine or undertake a similar flavoring process, you'll want to limit the time on the chips, etc., to avoid overdoing it.

There is one final argument in favor of racking your wine after the secondary fermentation completes, and that is easier bulk storage. This can be as simple as a space and/or time issue. If you don't need your wine for a while, for example, if you don't plan to drink it within two or three months anyway, or if you've made multiple batches and perhaps you're bottling one but don't need the second and don't have the room to store it, go ahead and rack it in a bulk bottle instead.

Follow the "rules" of storage (ahead in another section), keep it tightly sealed and in a cool, dark place, with minimal headspace, and save it for bottling later when you're closer to needing small bottled portions.

How much racking is too much racking?

Can you guess my answer here? There's no set number, but there are some good guidelines. And no, indefinite rackings is not the answer.

For country wines like ours that are not treated with sulfites and preservatives, I personally set the ideal number of rackings at two. As we talked about, the first will get your wine off the gross lees and into a carboy for secondary fermentation (this is the step where we strain the wine off the must after the first week and set it up in the jug to ferment and complete with the airlock). The second racking would come about a month after this and would be when you siphon the completed and cleared wine off the thick layer of fine lees that will be produced during the secondary fermentation. In practice it's not a lot different than the first racking (except that it's easier because it's just a matter of siphoning without all the straining and draining of removing the "gross lees" – gross meaning the net or total amount of lees, not disgusting...although, they are a little gross, and you'll be happy to see them fallen out of your wine). I would leave this wine to sit racked for a period of one to two months, at which time I would siphon the wine off the lees again, but then bottle it as opposed to racking it more times.

The reason I advise this for our particular brand of simpler, cheaper, cleaner wines is that this schedule of racking gives you the best balance of completeness and clarity without over-exposing your wine to air and oxidation and other environmental spoilage organisms. It's a good happy medium that doesn't put your wine in an unnecessarily risky position.

Of course, this is a guideline and the one I feel best suited for simplified, basic wine making, but you can create your own schedule of racking, too. A few rules of thumb to keep in mind are:

- Rack wine off lees within two months to avoid off-flavors from decaying yeasts.
- Rack wine off lees when there is more than one-half inch of lees in the bottom of the racking vessel (after secondary fermentation is complete – during secondary fermentation, leave undisturbed for the entire month). More than one-half inch of lees in later rackings allows enough of a layer for yeast to start to decay and impart off flavors.
- If you are performing flavoring such as oaking, rack the wine off the oak before the flavor becomes too overpowering – a subjective decision based on your own personal taste and goals for your wine.
- Multiple rackings can become too much of a good thing and make a good wine bad. Don't overdo it. Two rackings should be sufficient for un-sulfited country wines; three to four for wines with preservatives / sulfites.
- Once your wine is cleared and flavored there is no point in subsequent rackings and all you're doing is exposing it to negative elements like spoilage organisms and oxygen. When there are no significant lees to get it off of, seal the wine up until you can bottle it instead. It is perfectly fine to leave a well-sealed bulk bottle of wine to age for months (minimal headspace of course; see following). Once that bulk bottle is open, however, bottle the wine into sealed wine bottles to control air exposure.

Before we get into the actual process of how to rack your wine, let's consider one final point. If you're not quite sure whether to rack or bottle your wine, you do have a middle-of-the-road kind of option, and that is to do a little bit of bottling into wine bottles for earlier use and serving, and rack the remaining wine into a bulk wine storage vessel for another racking. For example, you could rack most of the wine into a smaller carboy, such as a three-gallon bulk jug, and then take the remaining gallon or two and bottle it into corked or capped wine bottles. The benefit here is that you can bulk-age most of the wine for clarity and finish and still have some to drink earlier on, while still limiting spoilage and air/surface exposure. This is something you could do whether it's your second, third, or subsequent racking...just be sure to fill those bottles up for the good of your wine.

HOW TO RACK YOUR WINE

Racking wine after the secondary fermentation is a simple process. All you will need is your siphon or long length of hose and a fresh, clean jug to rack into. If you only have one jug, you can also siphon into a clean fermentation bucket, cover it up, clean out the jug you've just siphoned from, and pour the wine back into it (clean it thoroughly, and get all those lees out).

All you need to do to rack your wine is to carefully set your hose or siphon end down into your wine so that it sits just above the sediment layer at the bottom. Don't set the hose too close to the sediment/lees—you want to avoid sucking up any of the lees if possible. DO NOT put your hose end into the lees! Your goal is to siphon the clear wine from above the lees so that only have clean wine in your new racking vessel. Yes, that means that you will be left with some murky liquid in the bottom of your fermenter when you are done and yes, you'll feel a little sad to waste that amount, but these things can't be avoided if you want good, clear wine in the end.

The racking process is really just siphoning the wine off the lees into a new vessel, doing your best not to expose the wine for too long to air and oxygen, and getting it sealed up in that new container with an air-tight cap as soon as possible. There is only one additional thing you need to consider before you do seal it up, and that is the amount of exposed surface area and headspace in the racked container.

As we've talked so much about already, the biggest spoilage factor for wine is air and oxygen. For aging wine, whether in a bottle or a carboy or bulk jug, we need to minimize the air available to the wine. The way we do this is by controlling the amount of headspace, or how much empty space is left at the top of the bottle. This is very important when you are racking wine in a large vessel, because even an inch or two down from the neck of the vessel leaves a lot of space for air and a large amount of the wine's surface in contact with that air, in addition to a large volume of wine that can all be spoiled and multiply the effects.

Your goal when racking is basically the same as it is when you are bottling into wine bottles. Fill the bottle up to the neck of the jug so that the wine just starts to fill the bottom of the neck. You'll need enough room left in the neck to sink your cork or stopper, if applicable, with just a small amount of empty space for liquid expansion so that you don't push the cork or stopper out when the wine goes through its normal process of expanding and contracting with environmental pressure and temperature. (Don't get too hung up on these things – just aim to fill your vessel to the bottom of the neck and leave it at that). The issue that winemakers often run into is that, because we lose an amount of wine and solids to the normal process of making wine and straining off the lees, we are often left with less wine at each additional racking, and you are likely to find yourself with a smaller amount of wine that will no longer fill up your vessel. Especially when you rack off the lees for the first time, you can lose a lot of volume – a gallon or more, even. But you do not want to be aging in a container that is only 75% full. You want – you *need* – to get that volume up to the bottom of the neck. So, what are you to do if you just don't have that much wine left and you are left with a large headspace and surface area?

When you are left with too much headspace in a fermentation vessel, you have a few options:

1. **Use a smaller jug or carboy.** There's no reason you have to use the jug or carboy that you started out with, except when you are trying to control the wine-making budget and you are trying not to invest in all the equipment under the sun. Those plastic water jugs are available in a range of sizes from one-half gallon up to five or six gallons and all sizes in between, for not a lot of money (online especially and from large retailers). Plan ahead and maybe invest in a cheap three- or four-gallon jug, depending on your anticipated need (you'll probably be able to

"eye-ball" your batch a week or so before racking and gauge what volume will roughly be lost to lees so you can order in what you'll need).

2. Break the wine down into two, three, or more bulk batches using smaller jugs or carboys. The idea here is to try to move the wine into smaller vessels that will fill the bottle up with the amount of wine you've produced; this is one of the better solutions but the problem is that you don't always have that option, and breaking down the batch into smaller carboys means that you need an even larger equipment supply (more money). It also means that when you do siphon and rack or bottle next time, you will probably lose a little more wine to the leavings when you siphon off those lees. You can also still be left with a quantity that doesn't quite fill the jug...so you're still left with an airspace/headspace problem, albeit, hopefully, reduced.

3. **Top up your jug with a similar wine.** At this point in the process, you don't want to keep adding water to your wine because it will dilute the completed wine further and throw off preservative alcohol levels. You can, however, add in another completed wine. Depending on what you use to top with, this may affect the flavor you've achieved, but it should be a more moderate effect and with a good choice of a "topping" wine, you should still be able to maintain good quality and body. The key is to choose a wine that is very similar to the wine you are producing. For example, for our favorite elderberry wine, I would probably use a nice cabernet.

The drawback to topping with another wine is that you do dilute the flavor and complexity profile a little bit and lose some of that 100% batch fruit wine flavor. It's a much lower impact than watering the wine down, though, and certainly better than losing your entire batch to oxidation and spoilage. One thing to keep in mind if you do top with another wine is that most commercial wines contain added sulfites, so if you are making your wine with an eye to a cleaner wine, you'll want to choose one that is labelled as having no added sulfites. Think similarly for any other practices or aspects that matter to you; organic, for example.

A better option to maintain the flavor of the wine you are making without compromising it by topping with a different wine is to top with a bottle or two of the same homemade wine – maybe one from your last batch, or last year's leftover bottle (if you have any around a year later...I don't ever seem to). Some people reserve previous bottles just for this purpose (what disciplined people they must be!). The benefit, however, is that you still have that completely homemade, start-to-finish wine made from all the very same ingredients, preserving the flavor and integrity of the batch.

4. **Top your wine with a space filler.** You can also solve this problem by taking up that headspace with a safe space filler. Small food-safe glass balls or marbles are perfect for this purpose. You can find these easily enough through wine-making supply vendors or online retailers. All you are doing here is filling the bottom of the jug with enough marbles to make the wine rise to the neck of the jug. Do sanitize the marbles beforehand and let them dry and take care when adding them to the jug to avoid chips and breaks – work slowly and drop a few in at a time (or if putting in before the liquid, try turning the bottle on its side and then slowly standing it up). Just to be on the safe side, when I do eventually bottle wine that has had a filler in it, I like to run the wine through a filter, such as a coffee filter or muslin cloth.

This is, hands down, my preferred choice for taking up headspace if I can't just go down a jug size and solve the issue by simply racking down. My wine stays pure and true to my intent of a clean, cheap, homemade wine that I know everything about; I don't add someone else's cheap wine and cheapen my good wine; I don't worry about their preservatives and sulfites; I don't add much to my cost; the marbles will be cleaned and put away to reuse another day, and so over time their cost to me is reduced; and I don't lose the flavor and balance of my wine that I've worked so hard to achieve. It's a simple, economical problem-solver that I'll now have on hand for a very common occurrence.

With your wine safely in its rack, making sure it is well-sealed against air infiltration, let it set mostly undisturbed in a cool and preferably dark place until you are ready to bottle it and use it (perhaps with an eyeball check-in here and there). This could be anywhere from a few weeks to a few months, taking into account those factors just discussed – timing your racking, bottling, time on lees, and so on.

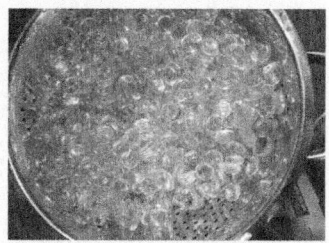

Glass marbles make a cheap, easy, reusable space-filler for late rackings to take up airspace without changing the integrity of the wine.

HOW TO BOTTLE YOUR WINE

There is really nothing complex about bottling your wine. Every winemaker probably has their own little tips and tricks and you're sure to find yours, too. As for the process of it, the biggest challenge is finding a way to efficiently get the liquid in the small mouth of the wine bottle. I usually do it one of two ways: I either use my siphon hose and just plug the end in between bottles, or I pour a large

Wine loves a cool, quiet, dark corner of a basement.

amount of wine into a handy drink container with a spigot on the bottom and bottle from there. Funnels and measuring cups work, too.

Whatever you have that works for you to get most of the wine into your stock of wine bottles without losing too much, and hopefully not aerating it too much.

How you get it into your bottles matters less than how you handle things in the process. Here are some of the more important points and some helpful tips to keep in mind when bottling your wine:

- Lay down some newspaper to catch drips and spills and make cleanup easier.
- Get out all necessary equipment including bottles, siphon, hose, funnel, corks, corker, caps, towels for cleanup.
- Clean, sterilize, and dry wine bottles and other equipment ahead of time. Even a day before isn't a bad idea to allow everything to dry properly. Here's a tip – wine bottles don't like to dry standing up, so invert them in a dishwasher rack or bottle rack or lay them on their side on a towel.
- To sterilize wine bottles for bottling, use one of the methods previously discussed. If your bottles fit safely in your dishwasher without banging around or hitting rotating spray arms or jets, a high heat or sterilization cycle is an excellent time-saver.
- Again, make sure your stopper and toppers, whether corks or caps, are ready and waiting. You just don't want to leave your wine out exposed to air any longer than is reasonable or necessary. It is perfectly fine to fill a case of bottles and then go back and cork or cap them, but you don't want uncapped wine to be hanging out all day.
- If this is your first time bottling, or even if it's just been a while and especially if you are working with new sizes of bottles and corks or stoppers, it's not a bad idea to familiarize yourself by filling and capping a bottle or two before you jump into the whole batch; this will help you get a feel for how full to fill your bottles and also ensure your corks or caps are the right size. Do a couple start to finish as a test.
- Soaking and sanitizing corks for a long period is not necessary and can end up breaking-down your corks. However, a short

soak of around 20 minutes in clean water does make corking with a hand-corker easier.

- Fill bottles until the wine just comes into the neck of the bottle. The idea is to leave just a little headspace (air space) without leaving so much that oxidation will be significant, but also leaving a little room for the wine to expand and contract as it will with environmental factors (temperature, pressure, etc.); this expansion is a normal factor in the best of storage situations and if you don't leave a little breathing room, you may end up with a lot of popped or pushed corks; not a good situation. You also want to reduce the surface area of the top of the wine as much as possible, and the way to do this is to get that liquid up into the smallest portion of the bottle.
- Be sure you leave enough room for corks to sink down into the bottle with a little room left for air/headspace. Until you've corked a few, it's easy to underestimate how much room the cork needs in the neck of the bottle. Again, try a few out ahead of time, find out where your mark lies, and use the first few as your guide.
- You may decide to use those nice shrink-wraps over the cork or wax the tops of the bottles, but neither is strictly necessary and plenty of us do not. The choice is yours.
- *DO* be sure to label your bottles with year and type/variety. Your label can be fancy, something you've printed on your computer (they do make printable bottling and canning labels for this), or ordered online; it can be a quick hand-written label on a mailing label; it can be masking tape; dissolvable are nice for future sanity for reusing bottles, but not a must. Just use *something*. You may think you'll know what's what six months from now, but you won't. Especially if you've caught the bug and moved on to trying this type of wine, and that type of wine...which is bound to happen. Label them!
- Find a friend. Wine is better with friends, isn't it? So is bottling and corking. With one filling and one corking, things can move along a lot more quickly and reduce the wine's time exposed to air.

STEP 7: AGE, STORE, ENJOY

A good place to store and age your bottled wines is essential. For unsulfited country wines, good storage, along with good bottling, is the key to preserving your wine for its best future enjoyment.

There is nothing complicated about storing your homemade wine. You simply need to look for the location in your house where 1) you are willing to store a large quantity of wine for a number of months to a year or years, and 2) it has the closest to ideal wine storage conditions for aging. Best conditions and temperatures for aging are different than the best temperatures for fermenting, and so this location should be different than where you actually "made" or fermented your wine.

Wine's Best Storage Conditions

Good storage is the key to preserving your efforts over the long term. There are a few things wine likes in terms of long-term home storage. It doesn't take a lot to establish these conditions, either. A little observation and effort are all it takes.

There are only a few criteria you are trying to meet in choosing where to store your homemade wine. Basically, you are looking for a cool, dark area that is maybe a little on the damp side and where the conditions don't change a whole lot over the span of time. Get as close to the "ideal" conditions as you can, but don't fret too much – close and fairly steady will be good enough. So, what is "ideal"?

> • **Ideal temperature.** To maintain the best quality in your wine, you want your wine to be kept cool. The best range is between 50- and 60-degrees Fahrenheit, with 55°F considered to be "the" ideal. Creeping up towards 70 and over is too high. Below 45 is too cool and probably too dry (see the discussion on humidity below). Certainly anywhere that the wine might ever freeze is a bad location – besides what it does to the wine's quality, freezing means expansion which can mean popped corks and broken bottles.

Temperatures on the colder side are preferable to temperatures on the warmer side. The consensus is that cooler temperatures slow the aging process down (here we're talking temperatures lower than 55°F). While there's a point where this might not be ideal for flavor and complexity formation, considering that your cleaner wines without added sulfites and stabilizers are some-what more vulnerable than chemically-balanced wines, erring on the side of cooler and slower aging for our style of wine is not a bad idea. (Worth a note: Very cool temperatures [usually under 50°F] can cause wines to produce crystals that look some-thing like rock candy. These are "tartrate crystals" and they are completely harmless. If you see them, do not think your wine is ruined. It's not. In fact, sometimes producers will do this purposefully because it helps to remove off flavors like vinegar tastes. If you see them, ignore them. Move on. Drink. Enjoy.)

• *Steady* **temperature control**. Of even more importance than hitting the perfect temperature mark is finding a location with a steady temperature. This should be a place where the tempera-ture doesn't fluctuate much day to day or month to month. That doesn't mean you will never see a degree or two or three of change, and that's okay. Just avoid large temperature swings and swings that rise too high on the ideal spectrum. Avoid frequent swings, such as daily or weekly. But if you see a moderate change, say from season to season that then evens out, and you're still comfortably in the range of good storage, don't sweat it. A temperature that changes a little but stays pretty consistent over a period of months is to be expected in a home environment and will really do no appreciable harm.

There are a couple of reasons why we aim for steady cool temperatures and above all, consistency. First, consistent cool temps help to avoid producing "cooked" flavors and "flatten-ing" of wine flavors. Secondly, and more importantly still, consistent temperatures help reduce expansion and contraction of the wine, the liquid itself. Note that you will never completely avoid expansion and contraction – it's a normal, natural, scientific occurrence; but when it happens, corks and covers can also expand and contract, pushed or pulled by the force, and that can allow some air and oxygen to be pushed or pulled in, and potentially cause a little seepage of wine. A limited degree of this expansion/contraction/push/pull air infiltration is pretty much expected and is not something to lose sleep over. The point is, though, that good conditions do limit the effect and help to protect and control the wine and its quality. It's a little point worth knowing just to know why it's worth finding a good resting home for that wine you've put so much work into.

• **Keep it in the dark**. Light breaks wine down and degrades its quality. This is true of any light source, but especially sunlight and UV rays. This is a big reason why wine is often bottled in dark-colored glass bottles, which gives it more light protection. Your storage room should be dark most of the time. If there are windows, try to get the wine as far away from them as possible. A little light when you are in the room won't end your wine world, but you should avoid having your wine in a well-lit or sunny room as much as possible.

• **A little humid is good.** An area that is a bit humid is beneficial; preferable, even. However, if you have to choose from a location that can meet either steady low temperatures or higher humidity but not both, let temperature be your determining factor. For wine storage, something around 60% humidity is the target, but anything in the range of 50-70% humidity or a little above is fine. The average comfortable humidity in most homes is about 40-50%; so if you think about the slightly more moist and less comfy areas of your home, like a more damp basement, those are probably good places to keep your wine (temperature and other factors considered). You don't really need to spend money to choose the most well-suited spot in your house, but if you do want a little help, you can purchase an inexpensive battery-operated digital thermometer with a humidity reading.

Higher humidity helps in storing wine because it keeps corks from drying out and therefore also helps to control that air seepage. Can it be too high? Not really for the wine itself, but areas with very high humidity can dampen and damage labels and allow mold to grow on the exterior of the bottles and on that labelling. If this happens, it doesn't ruin your wine but it might make your bottles less pretty and presentable, and you would certainly want to wash the bottles off before opening and serving so that you don't pour through and mix anything into the wine.

• **Standing tall or laying down?** Many of us think of bottles lying on their sides in a wine rack to be stored. Is that a definite necessity? The short answer is no. Storing bottles of wine on their sides has its benefits, but if your location and shelving don't allow for it, it's really not a must-do.

The reason that wine has traditionally been stored on its side (and it's actually on its side with the neck and cork pointed slightly downward), is that this fills the neck with wine touching the cork and helps to keep the corks from drying out. It would really take a very dry environment and a long time in storage before upright storage and cork dehydration became an appreciable problem, and your homemade wines most likely aren't going to be around that long, so again, this isn't something worth fretting over. Storing wine on a rack on its side does have other benefits, too, though, and space, storage, and retrieval are among them. Plus, there's something about a rack full of wine on its side that makes you feel accomplished. Storage racks do not need to be fancy and if you're handy one can be made easily. There are also some very good, reasonably-priced kits available through Amazon and other sellers.

• **Maybe avoid vibration.** And this is only a maybe because it's not a big factor and it's one that is open to debate. There is some debatable talk over whether vibration in the storage environment is a break-down factor. Certainly not even all the wine "experts" agree this is a big concern, but the idea is that constant vibration can speed chemical processes and prevent sediment from settling. While it seems sensible to find a nice, vibration-free location if you have one, if you find this to be difficult in the setup of your home it's not a factor worth stressing about.

• **Away from sources of fluctuation.** More important than worrying over vibration, look to avoid sources in the home that would cause your storage conditions to fluctuate a lot. We've already talked about the importance of maintaining a pretty steady temperature and ideally a fairly steady level of humidity, now think about whether anything in or near your storage area might cause a lot of disruption to desirable conditions there. Furnaces, heaters, air conditioning units, washers, dryers, dehumidifiers, ovens, appliances...these can all be sources of heat and cold and using them can change the environment of your wine storage daily.

In the home, the easy answer for wine storage is in a dark, steady, corner of your basement, away from your heating and cooling units and other major appliances, where it is probably the coolest and most humid. If you don't have a basement, maybe don't have the room, or something in the basement precludes it from long-term wine storage, your next best place to consider is something like a dark closet or corner of a cool pantry. Look for that spot just cooler than your average comfortable room temperature; a bit more moist, darker. The spot you don't love but that your wine will.

How Long to Age Homemade Wine

Here's what is really the hardest part of home winemaking: Waiting to enjoy the fermented fruits of your labors.

There's a notion drilled into us that you *must* wait months, *years*, on end before you can enjoy your wine. Since we are here to dispense with the "rules" that hold us back and keep us from this simple enjoyment, let's do away with this notion, too. It's said that even most commercially available wines are not really ideal for extended long-term storage (such as we'd think of for wine collecting and aging over time). Even these wines, sulfite-added and protected, are better enjoyed within the first few years of production. Therefore, the notion that you must sit and wait to enjoy your clean country wines for years on end is baseless.

Here's the bottom line. Once your wine has completed fermentation, there is no reason you can't drink it. It is now alcohol; the yeast has ceased acting; it. is. *wine*. Therefore, you are now talking just a matter of taste – flavor, development, complexity, and character. Are those bad things? Certainly not. If developing to reach a goal or complexity is what you're interested in, play with it. Age it. Sample along the way and note when you think the wine has hit its peak. But otherwise, just enjoy your bottles when you want to. Sommeliers may cringe, but too many rules suck the fun out of homemade and homesteading pursuits. Be safe, but then be free.

All of that said, here are a few guidelines to give you an idea of when you might most enjoy your simplified homemade wines:

- Wines can be drunk as early as one month old if the fermentation is complete. So, having a glass at the time of racking or bottling is just fine. In fact, it's helpful because over time and experience you get to learn a thing or two about the differences aging can make and it helps you develop a plan for making and aging wines that suit you.

- If we have to give it a timeline, three to six months is a good window for lighter country wines and berry wines. This gives them enough time to develop some good flavor without losing it to the natural processes of wine life.
- Darker wines benefit from a longer aging period of six months to a year. especially for your harsher dark fruits and berries (elderberry comes to mind here), a longer time aging helps to mellow the early harshness and smooth the rough edges.
- Wine rules would dictate that one to three years would be an even better base for aging before consumption, but for less-preserved wines, I err on the younger side have always been happy, and those resources that teach a more simplified version of winemaking tend to suggest the six-month to one-year range.
- There are no rules you must follow. Complete the fermentation. Enjoy at will.

Here's one final thought on simple winemaking and aging: If you think about it, you won't drink a three or five-gallon batch of wine all in one sitting (at least not without a LOT of help). That means some of those bottles will age more than others. That makes for a good opportunity to enjoy some young wines, age some wines, and just note along the way the differences aging makes, what you enjoyed and when you enjoyed it the most, and use that to guide aging for your future batches. You're likely to find that this differs with different types and styles of wine, too. If you liked your wine young, drink it young. If you think the bottles enjoyed later in their life were more enjoyable, age the next batch a bit more before breaking into it. Or do both. Once fermented, we have no rules here.

WILD GRAPE COUNTRY WINE, START TO FINISH PROCESS

With a thorough understanding of the process now under your belt, let's pare the process down to the basics to make it easier to follow. We'll use a basic wild grape country wine for our run-through process.

Step 1: Prep for the Process

Collect and sanitize your equipment. You will need: Strainers/colanders, 5-gallon primary fermentation bucket, masher and/or gloves for mashing, large stock pot (12 quarts+)

Step 2: Gather & Prep Your Ingredients

You will need about 18 pounds of wild grapes. Wash the grapes. Remove them from the stems. (You do not need to de-seed the grapes.)

Step 3: Make the Must

Crush the grapes to break them open. The goal is to break open and expose the fruit and release as much juice as possible. Work in smaller batches in a large kitchen bowl and dump the crushed batches into your clean fermenting bucket. Gloved hands, a kitchen masher, or, if you have one available to you, a fruit press works well.

Step 4: Primary Fermentation

Dissolve 10 pounds of sugar in warm water (1½ to 2 gallons of water); simmer and stir in a large stock pot until the sugar is completely dissolved. Let sit and cool. (You can do this before you begin crushing the grapes if you like, and that way it is cooling while you are working on the must and should be cool enough to use by the time you are done making the must.)

Add the cooled sugar water to the must in the 5-gallon fermenting bucket and stir through.

When the must/sugar-water mixture is about 100-105°F, put a couple of cups in a bowl and sprinkle the packet of yeast over the top of the must. Do not stir. Let the yeast sit and rehydrate for about 15 minutes, then stir. Next, check the bucket of must and make sure it is not hotter than 115°F, aiming more for a temperature between 85 and 100°F; then add the proofed yeast/must to the bucket and stir it through to distribute. If more liquid is needed, top up the bucket with warm water, but leave 4 to 5 inches of space at the top to leave room for the "cap" to rise over the next week.

Place your bucket in your designated primary fermentation location. Cover with a clean linen cloth or light plastic wrap with holes poked in it. *Do not* cover the bucket tightly – this is only for control of fruit flies and foreign matter dropping into the bucket. The must will need air to breathe for this step and will produce cover-exploding gases if tightly covered.

Stir the must every day to break up the cap and keep grapes and pulp incorporated.

Step 5: Straining & Secondary Fermentation

After a week, strain the must to remove the grapes, seeds, skins, and any other solid material. Strain the juice into a clean second bucket, and let drain until you have captured as much of the juice as possible. The result will be a murky, dark liquid.

Using a funnel, pour the strained liquid into a 4- or 5-gallon carboy (or water jug, whatever you are using). Top the liquid with luke-warm water, up to the neck or near to it, using your judgment; if you think it is too much added water, it is okay to stop a little short).

Add an airlock to the fermenter. It should be air-tight so that the carbon gasses and expelled air can escape, but outside air cannot get back in (see previous instructions). Place the racked young wine in your designated area for secondary fermentation (draft-free, limited light, steady temperature about 75 °F). Let sit for a month, checking periodically for signs of fermentation (bubbles rising in the jug, a growing layer of sediment on the bottom, bubbling in the jug or airlock).

Step 6: Racking and Bottling

Wait four weeks and look for signs of completed fermentation. When fermentation has stopped, either rack the wine for one to three months and then bottle (recommended) or move straight to bottling.

To rack the wine: Set your siphon hose down into the carboy towards the bottom of the jug, but above and not touching the lees (sediment). Avoid sucking up sediment as much as possible. Siphon wine into a clean carboy/jug/fermenter. Downsize the jug if necessary so that wine fills to the neck of the jug with little surface area and little airspace (alternatively, add clean, unbroken marbles to take up extra space in the bottom). Cover the jug tightly with a cap, stopper, etc. If desired, seal with tape to ensure no air seepage. Age in cool, dark aging area for one to three months and then siphon the wine off any new sediment and bottle.

To bottle the wine: Set your siphon hose down into the carboy towards the bottom of the jug, but above and not touching the lees (sediment). Avoid sucking up sediment as much as possible. If desired, run wine through a filter (coffee filters work well) to catch any accidentally siphoned sediment. You can siphon directly into bottles or into a large container and then fill bottles. Cork or cap bottles with air-tight caps. Move to cool, dark aging and storage area.

Step 7: Age & Enjoy

Store bottled wines in designated aging area (ideally, about 55°F, away from light and vibration, with around 60% humidity, with steady conditions). Enjoy at any time after completed fermentation. A recommended aging period for this wine would be from 3+ months.

Enjoy the fermented fruits of your labor!

6

MODIFYING WINE RECIPES

The following chapters will bring you both a bare-bones wine-making recipe and recipes for specific types of fruit and berry wines, all based on the cheap-and-easy method. But there is likely to come a day when you've whetted your wine-making appetite when you get looking at some gift or abundance of an available fruit or berry, or when you start wondering what this or that great tasty fruit, berry, or combination thereof might taste like in a homemade wine. Or, on that day, the thought may be that you'd really like to make wine with this or that amount of a gift or a harvest, but it's too little – or maybe too much – for the recipe you have on hand.

When these times come, it's good to know a little about how to modify a recipe, so that every abundance that comes your way has the opportunity to fulfill its wine destiny.

Frank Petersohn's recipe instructed us to "Find 15-20 pounds of something resembling fruit or vegetables." Vague? Perhaps, but the point is that Frank was never hung up on the minutiae and gave himself the flexibility to work with what he had and aim for a good wine with often great results, confidently knowing that wine at heart is not meant to be, nor does it need to be, a practice in stressful meticulousness to be successful. He believed it should be fun! Interesting! Creative!

The one thing to know about modifying a recipe for a batch of wine, whether up, down, or for fruit type, is that it is basically all about proportion. The elements in any wine recipe, you'll come to see, don't really vary all that much. This is more true of our simplified, cheap and easy wines because we are targeting a good wine we enjoy, not trying to replicate any wine to an exact standard (an act in futility anyway, as nature, growing years, conditions, and terroir play on the outcome, even for commercial producers). Our elements and ingredients are limited to the basics of fruit, water, sugar, and yeast.

There are basically four ways you might want to modify a wine recipe. You might want to adjust it to make a different size batch than what your recipe is supposed to make; maybe you have too much or not enough of the fruit, but still plenty to make a sizable batch and you need to balance the recipe to the amount of fruit you have on hand. You might want to substitute the fruit (or vegetable) to make a wine with what you have available; maybe you don't have blackberries, but you've got a bumper crop of raspberries. You might even want to combine fruits and flavors to create something unique, or to help stretch an otherwise low-quantity fruit to a batch size that is worth your while. And because we are focusing here on simplified, cheap and easy wines, you might want to modify a wine recipe to pare it down from a more complex, chemical-added version to one that fits our more basic method. Whatever your motivation, you should feel free to play and experiment. This is how new great wine flavors are found!

MODIFYING WINE RECIPES FOR BATCH SIZE

For any given recipe that you have, if you proportionally adjust the ratio of fruit to sugar to water, you can modify any recipe to make a larger or smaller batch. It's simply mathematics and percentages (though admittedly we all have times when our high school math memory fails us and those "simple" percentages don't seem that simple!). So maybe deal with it in easy terms...estimate to an easy one half or one-third batch and cut those numbers down accordingly. Just divide and reduce the numbers provided – or multiply to double or triple a small-batch recipe to grow it if that is the goal. As long as you keep the proportions of sugar and fruit and (to a lesser degree) the water the same, you'll turn a good batch of wine in any size. Keep in mind, though, most especially if you are *increasing* a batch size, that you can't work a batch larger than what your equipment can hold. If your fermentation jugs/carboys are five-gallon jugs, only work up to a five-gallon batch; if you still have a significant amount of fruit left, make a one- or two-gallon batch with the remainder.

The MOST IMPORTANT Thing to Know About Adjusting a Wine Recipe!

There is one very important, *most* important, thing to know about adjusting for recipe yield sizes. No matter how small a batch you are making, you **never reduce the amount of yeast to less than one packet**. Always use the equivalent of one packet of yeast, whether your batch is one gallon, two gallons, six gallons, or anything in between. If your batch will be larger than six gallons then you should use a second whole packet of yeast: One packet for every batch up to six gallons.

The reason that we never use less than the equivalent of one packet of yeast is that one packet of yeast is the *minimum quantity* needed to colonize a batch and multiply to a sustainable yeast level. (Wine yeast packets contain approximately a heavy teaspoon of yeast; bread yeast packets contain 2 ¼ teaspoons). After initial colony growth, fermentation and yeast viability is dictated by the food source (the sugar) and when the food is gone, the yeast goes dormant, no matter how much yeast there is. Yeast does not colonize and thrive dependent only on the amount introduced, but also by the environment and food and condition availability – and so in a manner of speaking the yeast controls itself, too, or lets itself multiply more with more food. Therefore using less than a packet might not give you enough to get the wine going and out-compete any nasty naturally-occurring yeasts that come in with the fruit...which would then make it that crapshoot we were trying to avoid by using a known yeast in the first place. This is why wine yeast producers will list the packet as enough to ferment between one and five/six gallons of wine – it's no mistake. For any size batch up to six gallons, use the whole packet and trust the yeast to do what it does naturally.

SUBSTITUTING FRUITS IN WINE RECIPES

Now let's suppose that the reason you need to modify your wine recipe is that you have an abundance of a certain type of fruit, but you don't have a recipe for that particular fruit wine. I have two options for you in this case.

Option one is easy – you can go to the bare-bones Basic Wine Recipe provided in the following chapter and plug your fruit into that recipe for the batch size you want to make. This will be dictated by the amount of fruit you have to work with and which size recipe most closely matches your quantity. This is a good solution, but you may end up with a wine that is slightly more or less sweet. This truly is a most basic recipe and the sugar quantity does not adjust to accommodate the specific fruit. It will still work with a good result, though.

The second option is to use a recipe that is designed for a similar fruit and substitute the fruit you have for what is called for. This option may give you a bit of a more honed result, assuming you are able to find a recipe for a fruit that closely matches what you are working with. If you decide to go this route, look for a fruit with a similar taste, sweetness, of a related family, etc.

MIX AND MATCH EXPERIMENTATION

Mixing and matching more than one fruit is also a good reason to play and modify a recipe. Maybe you don't have enough strawberries to turn out a good strawberry wine, but you have a good quantity of rhubarb to put with it and so you mix your two ingredients for a stellar strawberry-rhubarb wine; maybe you don't have enough raspberries, but you have a large combined quantity of raspberries, blueberries, and blackberries to make a mixed-berry wine. Whatever it is that you have on-hand, if you feel the flavors will complement each other, give it a try.

Again, in this case, you have two basic options. The first option is to mix the quantities of different fruits together to make up a full quantity to plug into either the Basic Wine Recipe or to substitute into another favorite recipe. If you choose this route, you probably want to use each type of fruit in equal measure to make up the total quantity of fruit needed. (Not necessarily, depending on what you're working with and your own discretion – if you feel it best to use more of an ingredient with weaker flavor, then go with your gut – it's an experiment, and it's up to you. That's the fun of it!). Your main concern will be to come up with enough *total* quantity for a batch. For example, 18-20 pounds of fruit is a pretty basic quantity for a five-gallon batch of wine. Let's say you're mixing raspberries and blackberries. My aim would be to use nine to ten pounds of each berry to make up the 18-20 pounds; but since raspberries have a more mild flavor, I also would not be shy about making the mix something more like 13 pounds of raspberries and 7 pounds of blackberries.

The second mix-and-match option is to make two different wines and mix the completed wines together at some time after the racking phase. In many ways, this is a safer option, only because you will have completed wines available to you which you can taste independently and then mix in experimental ratios to come up with the combined flavor just to your taste. This is very commonly done with grape wines and berries or fruits that have mild flavors when fermented, like cranberries and blueberries, for example. The grape helps to extend the quantity of less abundant (and often more expensive) fruits and berries, but it also helps to support the more subtle flavors and bring them out. A local New England vineyard does this when they produce their strawberry-rhubarb wine. They produce each wine separately and for a limited time (because they are natural and un-sulfited organic wines). They offer a strawberry wine and a rhubarb wine, but only for a period of a few months. After that time, they combine the two and offer strawberry-rhubarb wine (so you see, we cheap-and-easy home winemakers are not the only ones who want to play!).

The best way to go about doing this? Simple. Sit down with a completed bottle of each wine and a few glasses. Maybe a partner or a friend. Pay attention, maybe take down a note or two, and start mixing the wines in the percentages that you think will bring the best flavor. Fifty-fifty mix makes the most sense as a starting point, but if one wine is overpowering another flavor, you may need to make it something more like a 60%-40% split. Surely it will differ depending on what you are working to combine. If you're not sure how many tries you'll have to give it, you may want to use the taste-and-spit method of wine tasting. Mix and match responsibly! (Maybe plan to stay in that night.) The beauty of mixing and matching after you've made separate wines is that with a wine cellar full of options, you can create new wines any time you want, just by playing around a little.

SIMPLIFYING WINE RECIPES FOR CHEAP AND EASY WINES

There's probably going to come that day when you want to try a certain type of wine that you don't have a recipe for. So, you'll do a little digging, maybe online, maybe in some other wine book (it's okay – I won't feel cheated; information is for sharing). Quite often the recipe you'll come up with will be one that includes a lot of the additives that we aren't using here in this book. It may include tannins and sulfites and sorbates and yeast nutrients and acids and sometimes even things you might think are a little strange, like tea and raisins. You may choose to try some of those things out, or you may choose to just stick with the cheap and easy wine you've come to know and love. The question then becomes – how do you simplify a more complicated wine recipe?

Really, it's simple. The most important ingredients in the wine come down to only four things: Fruit or base ingredients, sugar (or sweetener such as honey), yeast, and water.

As long as you have these four things in proportion, you can just ignore everything else. Knowing these amounts is all you ever need to make a good batch of wine. It's just that easy.

CONVERTING QUANTITIES ACROSS COUNTRIES

Part modification/part information, knowing how to convert quantities and measures from one recipe to another is a good thing to know, too. Because of course, we do still have different systems and favored methods of weights and measures across borders. And of course, those systems aren't even the same exact measure. US, Imperial, Metric...the conversions are close, but just a little different.

So, what do you do if that perfect wine recipe is in a system of weights and measures foreign to you? Just follow the amounts listed below for converting from one unit of measure to another or hop online and find yourself one of those handy conversion calculators. Then take Frank's advice: *"...Give or take a pinch, imperial or US, who cares, it won't matter."*

...Because as we said, it's all about proportion and the yeast is a minimum quantity to start any amount of wine from one to six gallons anyway, so if you keep those proportions, you're going to come out just fine.

For simple, rounded, "close enough" conversions:

- 5 gallons = 20 liters
- 1 quart = 1 liter
- 2 pounds = 1 Kg
- 1 pound = .5 Kg
- 1 gallon = 4 quarts
- 1 gallon = 4 liters
- 1 pound of granulated white sugar = approximately 2 cups measured

If accuracy is your thing, these measures are more accurate:

- 5 gallons = 18.9 liters
- 1 quart = .95 liter

- 1 pound = .45 Kg

A NOTE ABOUT BACK-SWEETENING & FLAVORING WINE

Worth a mention, although this does not necessarily fit truly into the category of actual recipe modification, is the mention of back-sweetening and flavoring your wine with added extracts. We won't go in-depth into this topic because it somewhat pushes the boundaries of simple winemaking – it goes beyond the simplified start-to-finish batch and honestly, it's not an area in which I've much experience to offer; and so, we'll leave it as a topic we will brush upon to enlighten you to the possibilities if you choose to explore the topic further.

You may find that when you have made your batch of wine – and this is true of any wine, whether from a modified or adjusted recipe or not – that you'd like to enhance it through back-sweetening or flavoring. This might even be the case for the same wine recipe produced in exactly the same manner from one year to the next, because, as we've said before, the fruits and produce see different results from one year to the next. One year it might come out with a weaker fruit flavor profile; one year it might come out far more dry than you'd like.

If you do decide to try and "correct" for a flavor in a wine, you should start with sweetening it first. For example, before adding a fruit extract to boost a fruity flavor, back-sweeten the wine to taste (back-sweetening meaning to add in sugar in the form of simple syrup, *after* fermentation is completed and you know how dry the wine tastes). Sugar enhances flavors and brings weak flavors forward; judicious back-sweetening might be enough to get to the taste you desire. Back-sweetening should be done at the time of bottling, and it is recommended that you do add sulfite and potassium sorbate to the wine to stabilize it and prevent renewed fermentation...hence, we start to come away from the less treated, simple homemade wine and start venturing into more chemically-enhanced wines.

For a wine that comes out too sweet, there isn't a lot to be done except to take note and consider cutting back a sugar quantity in a subsequent batch, or perhaps mixing it with a dryer wine, either homemade or commercially produced. Of course, the same approach could be taken to "correct" a wine that has come out too dry if you happen to have a sweeter batch on hand. This is where that mix-and-match experimentation comes in handy.

Extracts can also be used to enhance a flavor and can be used either with a like fruit (raspberry for raspberry) or to subtly add to and enhance the flavor and complexity of a wine (think citrus to complement a blueberry wine, for example). Here too, then, you start to wander into the territory of additives, and depending on the extract you might be introducing artificial flavors. This is perfectly fine if you like, but if what you really want is an all-natural, minimal-ingredient cheap and easy wine, you may want to consider something more akin to the mix-and-match in the must or combining two clean varieties of wine. Once again, this is offered as an option worth exploring even though we don't cover it in-depth, just to make you aware of the possibilities so you can decide if this is a route worth exploring with your homemade wine. Since it is typically recommended to back-sweeten your wine and then add in extracts, again, you're likely to need to chemically stabilize the wine if you go this route.

One thing that you should understand about winemaking, especially winemaking in the more "country" style where you are using varieties of fruits and grapes that are not necessarily considered "wine" grapes and fruits, is that you cannot expect the result to be a fruity, juicy wine per se. Fermenting changes flavors and kind of sends fruit flavors to the background, resulting in more of an essence of the fruit than an actual fruity juice taste. Knowing and expecting this will give you a more realistic expectation of what your wine might taste like. (This is true of all fruit wines, including kits, those balanced with sulfites and acids, and commercial wines, too.) Understanding the goal might make you rethink whether you need to "correct" your wine or not. Both wine making and wine enjoyment are subjective; everyone will have an opinion. Make your goal making a wine that you enjoy, and then work towards that goal, and these corrections won't come much into play, anyway.

7

BASIC BARE-BONES WINE RECIPE AND AMOUNTS FOR COMMON WINES

Included in this chapter is the "bare-bones" wine recipe that has been referenced in the previous chapter. It is a very basic homemade wine recipe that will deliver a very good result, often great ("No, we don't sell this, but do sit and enjoy a glass with me."). It's not tailored or tweaked to any given fruit; it's primarily been constructed with grapes in mind but is versatile enough to work with most any fruit. This recipe is offered in the spirit of great simplified winemakers who have come before us – in the spirit of Frank Petersohn above all, and also in the spirit of resources like "Mother Earth News" and other supporters of simplified, old-time, basic wine making.

Using this recipe is simple. Input your desired fruit and follow the basic wine-making process. The recipe has been provided in three different batch sizes – five-gallon, three gallon, and one gallon. This makes this bare-bones recipe an easy reference for adjusting or substituting in recipes, and you can easily multiply smaller batch sizes to increase to a different size batch according to fruit availability (just remember not to multiply the yeast unless you make a batch larger than six gallons!).

Following the recipes, you will also find a basic wine-making chart for a variety of fruits and ingredients and the recommended amounts of sugar to use for various batches. Adjusting this bare-bones recipe with these more tailored fruit to sugar ratios will make for an even more tailored and balanced wine. Note that there are a number of vegetables that people use to make good wines, too, which may also be substituted for the "fruit" in these basic recipe formulas. Instructions are listed with the recipe amounts to provide a quick-glance refresher; refer back to the "process" instructions for more in-depth directions. Starting with clean equipment is assumed to be a "given" by now.

As always, it's also a good idea to take down some notes so that you can further adjust and tailor the recipe to your personal taste (a section for notes is included at the end of this book).

5-GALLON COUNTRY WINE RECIPE

- 18-20 pounds fruit
- 10 pounds sugar
- 4 gallons water, divided
- (more later for topping up for secondary fermentation)
- 1 packet yeast

Basic Instructions:

- Wash and destem fruit; deseed or de-pit if possible.
- Simmer the 10 pounds of sugar in 2 gallons of the water until dissolved. Set aside and let cool as you prepare the must.
- Crush fruit and release as much juice as possible. Work in batches so that all fruits or berries are equally destroyed.
- Place must of crushed fruit into a clean fermenting bucket, 5 gallons or larger.
- Add the sugar and water mixture and stir through.
- Ladle out about 2 cups of the warm must mixture into a small bowl or large measuring cup (making sure it's not too hot to

kill the yeast – between 100°F and 105°F). Sprinkle the yeast packet evenly over the top of the must. Rehydrate for 15 minutes, then stir. Let sit an additional 15 minutes until foamy.

- Add enough of the remaining water to the bucket of must to top up the volume. Leave about 4-5 inches at the top of the bucket to allow the cap space to rise without overflowing the bucket.
- Make sure the bucket of must is not too hot (ideally, around 85°F – you can add some cool water to help cool it down if necessary). Pitch the yeast/must mixture into the bucket of must and stir.
- Set the bucket in your designated fermentation area. Do not cover tightly (no lids – primary fermentation requires air); you may choose to cover loosely with a clean linen cloth.
- Let ferment for one week, stirring daily to break up the cap.
- After one week, strain solids and pour the liquid into a 5-gallon secondary fermenting jug or carboy. Discard fruit must. Top secondary fermenter with water until it reaches to the neck of the jug.
- Place an airlock on the secondary fermenter and leave undisturbed in your fermentation area for one month (check periodically to ensure the airlock has not dried out or has otherwise become compromised).
- After one month, check to see that secondary fermentation is complete. Siphon wine off the settled lees. Rack for one to three months more or bottle and store for aging and future use.

3-GALLON COUNTRY WINE RECIPE

- 10 to 12 pounds fruit
- 6 pounds sugar
- 3 gallons water, divided
- (more later for topping up for secondary fermentation)
- 1 packet yeast

Basic Instructions:

- Wash and destem fruit; deseed or de-pit if possible.
- Simmer the 6 pounds of sugar in 1 ½ gallons of the water until dissolved. Set aside and let cool as you prepare the must.
- Crush fruit and release as much juice as possible. Work in batches so that all fruits or berries are equally destroyed.
- Place must of crushed fruit into a clean fermenting bucket, (5-gallon size is good).
- Add the sugar and water mixture and stir through.
- Ladle out about 2 cups of the warm must mixture into a small bowl or large measuring cup (making sure it's not too hot to kill the yeast – between 100°F and 105°F). Sprinkle the yeast packet evenly over the top of the must. Rehydrate for 15 minutes, then stir. Let sit an additional 15 minutes until foamy.
- Add the remaining water, making sure there is room left in the bucket for the cap to rise without overflowing the bucket (at least 4-5 inches of space; more is fine).
- Make sure the bucket of must is not too hot (ideally, around 85°F – you can add some cool water to help cool it down if necessary). Pitch the yeast/must mixture into the bucket of must and stir.
- Set the bucket in your designated fermentation area. Do not cover tightly (no lids – primary fermentation requires air); you may choose to cover loosely with a clean linen cloth.
- Let ferment for one week, stirring daily to break up the cap.
- After one week, strain solids and pour the liquid into a 3-gallon secondary fermenting jug or carboy. Discard fruit must. Top secondary fermenter with water until it reaches to the neck of the jug.
- Place an airlock on the secondary fermenter and leave undisturbed in your fermentation area for one month (check periodically to ensure the airlock has not dried out or has otherwise become compromised).

- After one month, check to see that secondary fermentation is complete. Siphon wine off the settled lees. Rack for one to three months more or bottle and store for aging and future use.

1-GALLON COUNTRY WINE RECIPE

- 3 ½ to 4 pounds fruit
- 2 pounds sugar
- 1 gallon water, divided
- 1 packet yeast

Basic Instructions:

- Wash and destem fruit; deseed or de-pit if possible.
- Simmer the 2 pounds of sugar in 2 quarts of water until dissolved. Set aside and let cool as you prepare the must.
- Crush fruit and release as much juice as possible. Work in batches so that all fruits or berries are equally destroyed.
- Place must of crushed fruit into a clean fermenting bucket, 1 ½ to 2 gallons or larger.
- Add the sugar and water mixture and stir through.
- Ladle out about 2 cups of the warm must mixture into a small bowl or large measuring cup (making sure it's not too hot to kill the yeast – between 100°F and 105°F). Sprinkle the yeast packet evenly over the top of the must. Rehydrate for 15 minutes, then stir. Let sit an additional 15 minutes until foamy.
- Add enough of the remaining water to the bucket of must to make about one gallon in total volume. Make sure there is at least 3 to 4 inches of space at the top of the bucket to allow the cap space to rise without overflowing the bucket.
- Make sure the bucket of must is not too hot (ideally, around 85°F — you can add some cool water to help cool it down if necessary). Pitch the yeast/must mixture into the bucket of must and stir.
- Set the bucket in your designated fermentation area. Do not

cover tightly (no lids – primary fermentation requires air); you may choose to cover loosely with a clean linen cloth.

- Let ferment for one week, stirring daily to break up the cap.
- After one week, strain solids and pour the liquid into a 1-gallon secondary fermenting jug or carboy. Discard must. Top secondary fermenter with water until it reaches to the neck of the jug.
- Place an airlock on the secondary fermenter and leave undisturbed in your fermentation area for one month (check periodically to ensure the airlock has not dried out or has otherwise become compromised).
- After one month, check to see that secondary fermentation is complete. Siphon wine off the settled lees. Rack for one to three months more or bottle and store for aging and future use.

Chart: Ingredient Amounts for Common Wines

The chart below lists ingredient quantities for common fruits and ingredients for **5-gallon** batches of wine. Plugging these amounts into a basic bare-bones recipe will give you a wine that is a little more tailored to the specific fruits used as your base. Or....you can ignore this chart and simply go with the previous bare-bones recipes. Or...move on to the next chapter and find a dedicated recipe for your desired wine. It's all in the spirit of giving you the resources that work for you, and whatever route you choose, your wine is sure to be a success.

Common Amounts for 5-Gallon Wine Recipes

Type of Fruit	# of Pounds	Pounds of Sugar	Amount of Yeast	Approx. Amount Water to Start
Apple	35	8	1 packet	4 gallons
Apricot	18	13	1 packet	4 gallons
Blackberry	18	14	1 packet	4 gallons
Blueberry	12	14	1 packet	4 gallons
Cherries	14	12	1 packet	4 gallons
Chokecherries	13	13	1 packet	4 gallons
Crabapple	26	10	1 packet	4 gallons
Currant	15	13	1 packet	4 gallons
Elderberry	18	12	1 packet	4 gallons
Grapes	18	10	1 packet	4 gallons
Gooseberry	20	12	1 packet	4 gallons
Peach	18	12	1 packet	4 gallons
Pear	20	10	1 packet	4 gallons
Plum	13	12	1 packet	4 gallons
Raspberry	12	13	1 packet	4 gallons
Strawberry	13	8	1 packet	4 gallons

- 1 pound sugar = approx. 2 cups

Helpful metric conversions:

- 5 gallons = 18.9 liters
- 1 quart = .95 liter
- 1 pound = .45 Kg

Easier quick conversion amounts for the less exacting but a still great wine:

- 5 gallons = 20 liters

- 1 quart = 1 liter
- 2 pounds = 1 Kg

FAVORITE FRUIT WINE RECIPES (AND A FEW MORE FOR FUN)

If all you ever do is make wine using the chart and conversions provided in the previous chapter, or the bare-bones-and-substitute recipe, you will still turn out great wines. But if you'd like to try something a little more tailored, or perhaps something a little outside the box, the following favorite recipes are good places to start. To be sure, there are probably thousands (or more) recipes for homemade wines out there, and once you start fermenting, tweaking, and twisting, you'll have more to add yourself. With the previous recipes and charts and the following wine recipes, you'll have a very full complement of home wine-making recipes to fill your cellar.

Note: While some suggestions for yeast varieties are given in the recipes that follow, they are only that; suggestions. They are listed only to give you some guidance, but you should also feel free to exchange one yeast for another and/or to try a selection of your own. It is a good idea also to refer back to the chapter on yeasts or to consult the **Fast-Reference Wine Yeast Selection Chart** *for a refresher to determine whether the finer characteristics of a given yeast (such as reliability, temperature sensitivity, and vigor) might pose a challenge to you, in which case you may decide to opt for a more wide-ranging and reliable yeast. If this is all sounding like a headache to you, also feel free to* *do what I am probably going to do...pitch the all-purpose Montrachet/Premier Classique or just use the darn bread yeast!*

STONEWALL GRAPE WINE

MAKES 5 GALLONS

*suitable for use with cultivated grape varieties as well

In our house, we call this classic wild grape wine "Stonewall Grape" because our wild grapes grow largely along our New England stone walls, and they tend to take on the nose and subtle tastes of the local autumn terroir (my apologies for sounding so stuffy, but it's a fact). For us, it's like a breath of fresh New England fall air any time of the year, and one that every local equates with cooler days, autumn rains, and kids heading back to school (and isn't that always worth a glass or two?).

- 20 pounds wild grapes
- 10 pounds sugar
- 4 gallons water, divided
- (more later for topping up for secondary fermentation)
- 1 packet yeast
- (yeast suggestions: Bread/baker's yeast, Premier Classique, Premier Rouge)

Instructions:

- Wash and destem grapes
- Simmer the 10 pounds of sugar in 2 gallons of the water until dissolved. Set aside and let cool as you prepare the must.
- Crush grapes and release as much juice as possible. Work in batches so that all the grapes are equally destroyed.
- Place must of crushed grapes into a clean fermenting bucket, five gallons or larger.
- Add the sugar and water mixture and stir through.
- Ladle out about 2 cups of the warm must mixture into a small bowl or large measuring cup (making sure it's not too hot to kill the yeast – between 100°F and 105°F). Sprinkle the yeast packet evenly over the top of the must. Rehydrate for 15 minutes, then stir. Let sit an additional 15 minutes until foamy.
- Add enough of the remaining water to the bucket of must to top up the volume. Leave about 4-5 inches at the top of the bucket to allow the cap enough space to rise without overflowing the bucket.
- Make sure the bucket of must is not too hot (ideally, around 85°F – you can add some cool water to help cool it down if necessary). Pitch the rehydrated yeast mixture into the bucket of must and stir.
- Set the bucket in your designated fermentation area. Do not cover tightly (no lids – primary fermentation requires air); you may choose to cover loosely with a clean linen cloth to control fruit flies.
- Let ferment for one week, stirring daily to break up the cap.
- After one week, strain off the solids and pour the liquid into a 5-gallon secondary fermenting jug or carboy. Discard must. Top secondary fermenter with water until it reaches to the neck of the jug.
- Place an airlock on the secondary fermenter and leave it undisturbed in your fermentation area for one month (check periodically to ensure the airlock has not dried out or has otherwise become compromised).

- After one month, check to see that secondary fermentation is complete. Siphon the wine off the settled lees. Rack for one to three months more or bottle and store for aging and future use.
- Wild grape wine typically benefits from an aging period of one to two months, but then is often best enjoyed within a year of bottling.

BLACKBERRY WINE

MAKES 1 GALLON

For ease of use, this blackberry wine recipe is given in both a one-gallon batch size and, following, in a five-gallon batch size. Blackberries can be difficult to pick or obtain in quantities large enough for a full five gallons. However, it is not uncommon to find yourself with a good quantity, especially in a good berry year, of something that can make a batch in between. Thus, it is helpful to have both the smaller one-gallon batch size that multiplies easily as well as a quick-grab five-gallon batch for those of you blessed with local abundance. It is a forgiving and consistent country wine recipe, easier than many to prepare, with reliable results. This is an excellent wine recipe for the beginner.

- 3 pounds blackberries
- 2 ½ pounds sugar
- 1 gallon water, divided
- 1 packet yeast
- (yeast suggestions: Bread/baker's yeast, Premier Classique, Premier Rouge)

Basic Instructions:

- Wash and drain blackberries.
- Simmer the 2 ½ pounds of sugar in 2 quarts of water until dissolved. Set aside and let cool as you prepare the must.
- Crush the berries and release as much juice as possible. Work in batches so that all berries are equally destroyed.
- Place the must of crushed berries into a clean fermenting bucket, 1 ½ to 2 gallons or larger.
- Add the sugar and water mixture and stir through.
- Ladle out about 2 cups of the warm must mixture into a small bowl or large measuring cup (making sure it's not too hot to kill the yeast – between 100°F and 105°F). Sprinkle the yeast packet evenly over the top of the must. Rehydrate for 15 minutes, then stir. Let sit an additional 15 minutes until foamy.
- Add enough of the remaining 2 quarts of water to the bucket of must to make about one gallon in total volume. Make sure there is at least 3 to 4 inches of space at the top of the bucket to allow the cap enough space to rise without overflowing the bucket.
- Make sure the bucket of must is not too hot (ideally, around 85°F – you can add cool water to help cool it down if necessary and space allows). Pitch the yeast/must mixture into the bucket of must and stir.
- Set the bucket in your designated fermentation area. Do not cover tightly (no lids – primary fermentation requires air); you may choose to cover loosely with a clean linen cloth.
- Let ferment for one week, stirring daily to break up the cap.
- After one week, strain the solids off and pour the liquid into a 1-gallon secondary fermenting jug. Discard the fruit must. Top the secondary fermenter with water until it reaches to the neck of the jug (if needed).
- Place an airlock on the secondary fermenter and leave undisturbed in your fermentation area for one month (check periodically to ensure the airlock has not dried out or has otherwise become compromised).

- After one month, check to see that secondary fermentation is complete. Siphon the wine off the settled lees. Rack for one to three months more or bottle and store for aging and future use.
- Blackberry wine typically benefits from a short aging period but may be enjoyed any time after secondary fermentation is complete.

BIG-BATCH BLACKBERRY WINE

MAKES 5 GALLONS

- 15-18 pounds blackberries
- 12 pounds sugar
- 4 gallons water, divided
- (more later for topping up for secondary fermentation)
- 1 packet yeast
- (yeast suggestions: Bread/baker's yeast, Premier Classique, Premier Rouge)

Instructions:

- Wash and drain blackberries.
- Simmer the sugar in 2 gallons of the water until dissolved. Set aside and let cool as you prepare the must.
- Crush berries and release as much juice as possible. Work in batches so that all the blackberries are equally destroyed.
- Place must of crushed berries into a clean fermenting bucket, five gallons or larger.
- Add the sugar and water mixture and stir through.
- Ladle out about 2 cups of the warm must mixture into a small bowl or large measuring cup (making sure it's not too hot to

kill the yeast – between 100°F and 105°F). Sprinkle the yeast packet evenly over the top of the must. Rehydrate for 15 minutes, then stir. Let sit an additional 15 minutes until foamy.

- Add enough of the water to the bucket of must to top up the volume. Leave about 4-5 inches at the top of the bucket to allow the cap enough space to rise without overflowing the bucket.
- Make sure the bucket of must is not too hot (ideally, around 85°F – if there is room you can add some cool water to help cool it down if necessary). Pitch the yeast/must mixture into the bucket of must and stir.
- Set the bucket in your designated fermentation area. Do not cover tightly (no lids – primary fermentation requires air); you may choose to cover loosely with a clean linen cloth.
- Let ferment for one week, stirring daily to break up the cap.
- After one week, strain off the solids and pour the liquid into a 5-gallon secondary fermenting jug or carboy. Discard fruit must. Top secondary fermenter with water until it reaches to the neck of the jug.
- Place an airlock on the secondary fermenter and leave undisturbed in your fermentation area for one month (check periodically to ensure the airlock has not dried out or has otherwise become compromised).
- After one month, check to see that secondary fermentation is complete. Siphon wine off the settled lees. Rack for one to three months more or bottle and store for aging and future use.
- Blackberry wine benefits from a short aging period but may be enjoyed any time after secondary fermentation is complete.

RED RASPBERRY WINE

MAKES 3 GALLONS

Much like blackberries, raspberries can be a bit difficult to come by in quantity, particularly if you are picking from the wild. And so, this Red Raspberry wine recipe is given in a smaller batch size of three gallons along with the more common five-gallon batch size. (For a smaller one-gallon batch, just divide down). Remember that there is no harm in freezing smaller quantities of small-harvest berries until you have enough to work your batches – a trick that is particularly helpful with wild raspberries and blackberries that like to stretch out a ripening phase!

- 7-8 pounds raspberries
- 8 pounds sugar
- 3 gallons water, divided
- (more later for topping up for secondary fermentation)
- 1 packet yeast
- (yeast suggestions: Bread/baker's yeast, Premier Classique, Premier Rouge)

Instructions:

- Wash and drain raspberries.
- Simmer the sugar in 1 ½ gallons of the water until dissolved. Set aside and let cool as you prepare the must.
- Crush the berries and release as much juice as possible. Work in batches so that all berries are equally destroyed.
- Place the must of crushed berries into a clean fermenting bucket, (five-gallon size is good).
- Add the sugar and water mixture and stir through.
- Ladle out about 2 cups of the warm must mixture into a small bowl or large measuring cup (making sure it's not too hot to kill the yeast – between 100°F and 105°F). Sprinkle the yeast packet evenly over the top of the must. Rehydrate for 15 minutes, then stir. Let sit an additional 15 minutes until foamy.
- Add the remaining 1 ½ gallons of water, making sure there is room left in the bucket for the cap to rise without overflowing the bucket (at least 4-5 inches of space; more is fine).
- Make sure the bucket of must is not too hot (ideally, around 85°F – you can add some cool water to help cool it down if necessary and space/volume allows). Pitch the foamed yeast/must mixture into the bucket of must and stir.
- Set the bucket in your designated fermentation area. Do not cover tightly (no lids – primary fermentation requires air); you may choose to cover loosely with a clean linen cloth.
- Let ferment for one week, stirring daily to break up the cap.
- After one week, strain off the solids and pour the liquid into a 3-gallon secondary fermenting jug or carboy. Discard the fruit must. Top secondary fermenter with water until it reaches to the neck of the jug.
- Place an airlock on the secondary fermenter and leave undisturbed in your fermentation area for one month (check periodically to ensure the airlock has not dried out or has otherwise become compromised).
- After one month, check to see that secondary fermentation is

complete. Siphon wine off the settled lees. Rack for one to three months more or bottle and store for aging and future use.

- Raspberry wine benefits from a short aging period (about two months) but may be enjoyed at any time after secondary fermentation is complete.

BIG-BATCH RED RASPBERRY WINE

MAKES 5 GALLONS

Worthy of a second note, these red raspberry wine recipes would also be good for use with black raspberries or loganberries, should you be fortunate enough to have them!

- 13-14 pounds raspberries
- 13 pounds sugar
- 4 gallons water, divided
- (more later for topping up for secondary fermentation)
- 1 packet yeast
- (yeast suggestions: Bread/baker's yeast, Premier Classique, Premier Rouge)

Instructions:

- Wash and drain raspberries.
- Simmer the 13 pounds of sugar in 2 gallons of the water until dissolved. Set aside and let cool as you prepare the must.
- Crush raspberries and release as much juice as possible. Work in batches so that all fruits or berries are equally destroyed.

- Place must of crushed fruit into a clean fermenting bucket, five gallons or larger.
- Add the sugar and water mixture and stir through.
- Ladle out about 2 cups of the warm must mixture into a small bowl or large measuring cup (making sure it's not too hot to kill the yeast – between 100°F and 105°F). Sprinkle the yeast packet evenly over the top of the must. Rehydrate for 15 minutes, then stir. Let sit an additional 15 minutes until foamy.
- Add enough of the remaining water to the bucket of must to top up the volume. Leave about 4-5 inches at the top of the bucket to allow the cap space to rise without overflowing the bucket.
- Make sure the bucket of must is not too hot (ideally, around 85°F – you can add some cool water to help cool it down if necessary if space/volume allow). Pitch the yeast/must mixture into the bucket of must and stir.
- Set the bucket in your designated fermentation area. Do not cover tightly (no lids – primary fermentation requires air); you may choose to cover loosely with a clean linen cloth.
- Let ferment for one week, stirring daily to break up the cap.
- After one week, strain solids and pour the liquid into a 5-gallon secondary fermenting jug or carboy. Discard fruit must. Top secondary fermenter with water until it reaches to the neck of the jug.
- Place an airlock on the secondary fermenter and leave undisturbed in your fermentation area for one month (check periodically to ensure the airlock has not dried out or has otherwise become compromised).
- After one month, check to see that secondary fermentation is complete. Siphon the wine off the settled lees. Rack for one to three months more or bottle and store for aging and future use.
- Raspberry wine benefits from a period of short fermentation of about two months but may be enjoyed any time after secondary fermentation is complete.

COUNTRY BLUEBERRY WINE

MAKES 5 GALLONS

Blueberry wine is another berry favorite that is easy, basic, and good for beginners. And an equally good choice for more experienced winemakers because it is delicious. Keep in mind that, as is true of all fruits, you can always work from a stored/frozen supply and since all berries break down quite a lot in the freezing and thawing process, doing so does a lot of the work of crushing and juicing for you. It also makes it easier to pick and forage and build up that supply over weeks of ripening.

- 14 pounds blueberries
- 13 pounds sugar
- 4 gallons water, divided
- (more later for topping up for secondary fermentation)
- 1 packet yeast
- (yeast suggestions: Bread/baker's Active Dry yeast, Premier Classique, EC-1118)

Instructions:

- Wash and destem blueberries.

- Simmer the 13 pounds of sugar in 2 gallons of the water until dissolved. Set aside and let cool as you prepare the must.
- Crush berries and release as much juice as possible. Work in batches so that all berries are equally destroyed.
- Place the must of crushed berries into a clean fermenting bucket, five gallons or larger.
- Add the sugar and water mixture and stir through.
- Ladle out about 2 cups of the warm must and sugar water mixture into a small bowl or large measuring cup. Make sure it's not too hot to kill the yeast – between 100°F and 105°F; if hotter, allow to cool before proceeding. Sprinkle the yeast packet evenly over the top of the bowl of must. Rehydrate for 15 minutes, then stir. Let sit an additional 15 minutes until foamy.
- Add enough of the remaining water to the bucket of must to top up the volume. Leave about 4-5 inches at the top of the bucket to allow the cap space to rise without overflowing the bucket.
- Make sure the bucket of must is not too hot (ideally, around 85°F – if space allows you can add some cool water to help cool it down if necessary). Pitch the yeast/must mixture into the bucket of must and stir.
- Set the bucket in your designated fermentation area. Do not cover tightly (no lids – primary fermentation requires air); you may choose to cover loosely with a clean linen cloth.
- Let ferment for one week, stirring daily to break up the cap.
- After one week, strain off the solids and pour the liquid into a 5-gallon secondary fermenting jug or carboy. Discard fruit must. Top secondary fermenter with water until it reaches to the neck of the jug.
- Place an airlock on the secondary fermenter and leave undisturbed in your fermentation area for one month (check periodically to ensure the airlock has not dried out or has otherwise become compromised).
- After one month, check to see that secondary fermentation is

complete. Siphon wine off the settled lees. Rack for one to three months more or bottle and store for aging and future use.

- Blueberry wine benefits most from an aging period of two to three months before drinking (but is safe to drink any time after secondary fermentation is complete).

ROSÉ-STYLED STRAWBERRY TABLE WINE

MAKES 5 GALLONS

Strawberry wine is one that is said to be worthy and worthwhile across all methods, recipes, and styles of wine making. Even "lesser" strawberry wines are very good. What's more, the berries are very easy to work with, requiring little in the way of preparation, and fairly easy to access in suitable quantity for large batches of wine (and if you make it, do yourself a favor and make a large batch – anything less will leave you wanting). Strawberry wine undergoes a slightly longer maceration period that helps to extract the juices without a lot of crushing and handling – a few extra hours, but quite a lot less work.

Something else you will notice about strawberry wine recipes is that they can vary quite a bit in terms of fruit and sugar quantities. This results in a range of styles of strawberry wines, from light table-type wines to fuller, heavier, dessert-type wines. To that end, two different strawberry wine recipes are given here, and you can choose what seems most suited to you...or maybe what's most suited to your fruit supply! The first here is the lighter of the two, something more similar to a rosé, considered a lighter "table" wine, but equally up to the task of light sipping enjoyment with or without a meal.

- 13 pounds strawberries

- 8 pounds sugar
- 4 gallons water, divided
- (more later for topping up for secondary fermentation)
- 1 packet yeast
- (yeast suggestions: Bread/baker's Active Dry yeast, Premier Classique, Premier Blanc)

Instructions:

- Wash and drain berries. Cut tops off strawberries. Cut strawberries in half; quarter large berries.
- Work in two layers to prepare the berries: After about half of the strawberries are prepped and in the bucket, pour half of the sugar over the berries (do not dissolve the sugar in the water for this recipe). Continue preparing the rest of the strawberries and make a second layer, ending with pouring the remaining sugar over the top of the strawberries.
- Let prepped and layered strawberries stand for several hours to macerate (even overnight or up to 24 hours). During this process the sugars will draw the juices out of the strawberries and dissolve in the drawn juice. You can stir the mixture after several hours to further dissolve the sugar.
- When ready to proceed and prep for fermentation, you may crush the berries if you think they need it, though they will breakdown further as they ferment and this isn't strictly necessary.
- Ladle out about 2 cups of the strawberry juice into a small bowl or large measuring cup. Add a little warm water to make a warm juice that is not warmer than 105°F. Sprinkle the yeast over the top of the bowl of must. Rehydrate for 15 minutes, then stir. Let sit an additional 15 minutes until foamy.
- Add warm water to the bucket of juice and must (if necessary) to top up the volume in the bucket. Do not fill the bucket too full – leave about 4 to 5 inches of space at the top of the bucket to allow space for the cap to rise as it ferments.
- Make sure the bucket of must is not too hot (ideally, around

85°F). Pitch the proofed yeast/must mixture into the bucket of must and stir.

- Set the bucket in your designated fermentation area. Do not cover tightly (no lids – primary fermentation requires air); you may choose to cover loosely with a clean linen cloth.
- Let ferment for one week, stirring daily to break up the cap.
- After one week, strain off the solids and pour the liquid into a 5-gallon secondary fermenting jug or carboy. Discard fruit must. Top the secondary fermenter with water until it reaches to the neck of the jug.
- Place an airlock on the secondary fermenter and leave undisturbed in your fermentation area for one month (check periodically to ensure the airlock has not dried out or has otherwise become compromised).
- After one month, check to see that secondary fermentation is complete. Siphon wine off the settled lees. Rack for one to three months more or bottle and store for aging and future use.
- Strawberry wine benefits from an aging period of 3 to 6 months but can be enjoyed any time after secondary fermentation is complete.

COUNTRY-STYLED STRAWBERRY DESSERT WINE

MAKES 5 GALLONS

For a fuller-bodied, fuller-flavored, more dessert-style strawberry wine, try this recipe. Just right for sipping on an evening after dinner on a warm summer's eve...if you can get it to last from one summer to the next!

- 25 pounds strawberries
- 12 pounds sugar
- 4 gallons water, divided
- (more later for topping up for secondary fermentation)
- 1 packet yeast
- (yeast suggestions: Bread/baker's Active Dry yeast, Premier Classique, Premier Blanc)

Instructions:

- Wash and drain berries. Cut tops off strawberries. Cut strawberries in half; quarter large berries.
- Work in two layers to prepare the berries: After about half of the strawberries are prepped and in the bucket, pour half of the sugar over the berries (do not dissolve the sugar in the

water for this recipe). Continue preparing the rest of the strawberries and make a second layer, ending with pouring the remaining sugar over the top of the strawberries.

- Let prepped and layered strawberries stand for several hours to macerate (even overnight or up to 24 hours). During this process the sugars will draw the juices out of the strawberries and dissolve in the drawn juice. You can stir the mixture after several hours to further dissolve the sugar.
- When ready to proceed and prep for fermentation, you may crush the berries if you think they need it, though they will breakdown further as they ferment and this isn't strictly necessary.
- Ladle out about 2 cups of the strawberry juice into a small bowl or large measuring cup. Add a little warm water to make a warm juice that is not warmer than 105°F. Sprinkle the yeast over the top of the bowl of must. Rehydrate for 15 minutes, then stir. Let sit an additional 15 minutes until foamy.
- Add warm water to the bucket of juice and must (if necessary) to top up the volume in the bucket. Do not fill the bucket too full – leave about 4 to 5 inches of space at the top of the bucket to allow space for the cap to rise as it ferments.
- Make sure the bucket of must is not too hot (ideally, around 85°F). Pitch the proofed yeast/must mixture into the bucket of must and stir.
- Set the bucket in your designated fermentation area. Do not cover tightly (no lids – primary fermentation requires air); you may choose to cover loosely with a clean linen cloth.
- Let ferment for one week, stirring daily to break up the cap.
- After one week, strain off the solids and pour the liquid into a 5-gallon secondary fermenting jug or carboy. Discard fruit must. Top the secondary fermenter with water until it reaches to the neck of the jug.
- Place an airlock on the secondary fermenter and leave undisturbed in your fermentation area for one month (check periodically to ensure the airlock has not dried out or has otherwise become compromised).

- After one month, check to see that secondary fermentation is complete. Siphon wine off the settled lees. Rack for one to three months more or bottle and store for aging and future use.
- Strawberry wine benefits from an aging period of 3 to 6 months but can be enjoyed any time after secondary fermentation is complete.

RHUBARB WINE

Rhubarb is easy to grow, easy to prepare in quantity, and makes a nice, light country wine. It follows a similar process of maceration to strawberry wine. You can start rhubarb wine from fresh-picked stalks, but here's a tip – if you freeze the rhubarb first, even just overnight, it will help the cell walls break down and release more juice (freezing also makes rhubarb a good candidate for off-season wine making when you might have more time...although there is something about making rhubarb wine in June that just says "summer!").

- 20-25 pounds rhubarb stalks (never use the poisonous leaves, just the stems!)
- 11 pounds sugar
- 4 gallons water, divided
- (more later for topping up for secondary fermentation)
- 1 packet yeast
- (yeast suggestions: Bread/baker's yeast, Premier Classique, Premier Blanc, K1-V1116, EC-1118)

Instructions:

- Wash and drain rhubarb stalks; chop into ¼-½ inch pieces.
- Macerate the rhubarb in the primary fermenting bucket for 24 to 48 hours (in a cool place or refrigerator if for an extended period of time to prevent mold formation): Place half of the chopped rhubarb in the bucket and cover with half of the sugar. Repeat the layer with the remaining rhubarb and the remaining sugar, ending with the sugar. Cover with a loose lid or towel for a day or two; the sugar will draw the juice from the rhubarb. You can stir the mixture after several hours to further dissolve the sugar.
- Ladle out about 2 cups of the sugary rhubarb juice into a small bowl or large measuring cup. Add a little warm water to make a warm juice that is not warmer than 105°F. Sprinkle the yeast over the top of the bowl of must. Rehydrate for 15 minutes, then stir. Let sit an additional 15 minutes until foamy.
- Add warm water to the bucket of juice and must to top up the volume in the bucket. Make sure the liquid level at least covers the rhubarb pieces but do not fill the bucket too full – leave about 4 to 5 inches of space at the top of the bucket to allow space for the cap to rise as it ferments.
- Make sure the bucket of must is not too hot (ideally, around 85°F). Pitch the proofed yeast/must mixture into the bucket of must and stir.
- Set the bucket in your designated fermentation area. Do not cover tightly (no lids – primary fermentation requires air); you may choose to cover loosely with a clean linen cloth.
- Let ferment for one week, stirring daily to break up the cap.
- After one week, strain off the solids and pour the liquid into a 5-gallon secondary fermenting jug or carboy. Discard rhubarb must. Top the secondary fermenter with water until it reaches to the neck of the jug.
- Place an airlock on the secondary fermenter and leave undisturbed in your fermentation area for one month (check

periodically to ensure the airlock has not dried out or has otherwise become compromised).

- After one month, check to see that secondary fermentation is complete. Siphon wine off the settled lees. Rack for one to three months more or bottle and store for aging and future use.
- Rhubarb wine can sometimes be difficult to clear and may need a second or even third racking. It benefits from an aging period of 3 to 6 months but can be enjoyed any time after secondary fermentation is complete.

BLENDED STRAWBERRY-RHUBARB WINE

If you're anything like my household, strawberry-rhubarb anything is a no-brainer. Pie, a given. Crisp, a simpler stand-in. Jam for the off-season. Muffins, coffee cakes...I'm not sure there's anything strawberries and rhubarb can't improve. And wine? Say no more. In fact, the only issue I've ever had with strawberry-rhubarb anything is that there never seems to be enough of either to go around. And that is *certainly* true of strawberry-rhubarb wine.

**Worth a note! Strawberries are not the only thing with which rhubarb blends well. Raspberries are popular contenders and I can speak for blueberry-rhubarb jam combinations from personal experience. Former clients of mine from the land down under had never heard of strawberries and rhubarb together [though were not sad to do so] but said they use apples and rhubarb in combination all the time. In fact, if you have an abundance of rhubarb around, it's a good way to stretch some of these other fruits and berries in baking; and winemaking! Consider the options and the available options and if you decide to work other rhubarb combinations, follow along with these instructions and substitute in place of the strawberry(ies).

There are a couple of different options for making a combination strawberry-rhubarb wine; which you prefer, well that's really up to you. The first of the two options is to mix and blend together two separate strawberry and rhubarb wines. As in, make each wine separately to completion, then "bench test" and blend the two together.

Blending the two wines can be done at any time after secondary fermentation is complete. It is probably best to do this prior to bottling. Blend the wines to your taste (and maybe with a friend or significant other) by first mixing a few different ratios in a few small glasses. A 50/50 mix seems a reasonable place to start and balance the two, much like the famed strawberry-rhubarb pie: One part strawberry to one part rhubarb. A lot of winemakers like to bring the strawberry flavor forward and mix a 60/40 blend of 3 parts strawberry to 2 parts rhubarb. As said, it's just personal taste at this point and given differences year to year, you might even change it up between one season's wine and the next.

One of the biggest benefits to making strawberry-rhubarb wine by blending separate complete wines is that you end up with three distinct wines with only two fermentation processes. Another is that you can balance and blend until you arrive at just the right taste – just take care that you don't "balance and blend" too much or you might end up thinking they're all spectacular!

You can also make strawberry-rhubarb wine by fermenting the strawberries and rhubarb together in a single start-to-finish recipe. The benefit here being one batch, one flavor and also being able to make a batch with half of each ingredient; so, if quantities are low, this might be your way to go. The recipe for the combination fermentation follows.

ROSÈ-STYLE STRAWBERRY-RHUBARB WINE

MAKES 5 GALLONS

- 10 pounds strawberries
- 10 pounds rhubarb
- 10 pounds sugar
- 4 gallons water, divided
- (more later for topping up for secondary fermentation)
- 1 packet yeast
- (yeast suggestions: Bread/baker's yeast, Premier Classique, Premier Blanc, K1-V1116, EC-1118)

Instructions:

- Wash and drain rhubarb stalks; chop into ¼-½ inch pieces.
- Wash and drain strawberries; trim tops and half or quarter berries.
- Mix strawberries and rhubarb together.
- Macerate the strawberries and the rhubarb in the primary fermenting bucket for up to 24 to 48 hours (in a cool place or refrigerator if for an extended period of time to prevent mold formation): Place half of the chopped berries and rhubarb in

the bucket and cover with half of the sugar. Repeat the layer with the remaining berries and rhubarb and the remaining sugar, ending with the sugar. Cover with a loose lid or towel for a day or two; the sugar will draw the juice from the strawberries and rhubarb. You can stir the mixture after several hours to further dissolve the sugar.

- Ladle out about 2 cups of the sugary juice into a small bowl or large measuring cup. Add a little warm water to make a warm juice that is not warmer than 105°F. Sprinkle the yeast over the top of the bowl of must. Rehydrate for 15 minutes, then stir. Let sit an additional 15 minutes until foamy.
- Add warm water to the bucket of juice and must to top up the volume in the bucket. Make sure the liquid level at least covers the strawberry and rhubarb pieces but do not fill the bucket too full – leave about 4 to 5 inches of space at the top of the bucket to allow space for the cap to rise as it ferments.
- Make sure the bucket of must is not too hot (ideally, around 85°F). Pitch the proofed yeast/must mixture into the bucket of must and stir.
- Set the bucket in your designated fermentation area. Do not cover tightly (no lids – primary fermentation requires air); you may choose to cover loosely with a clean linen cloth.
- Let ferment for one week, stirring daily to break up the cap.
- After one week, strain off the solids and pour the liquid into a 5-gallon secondary fermenting jug or carboy. Discard must. Top the secondary fermenter with water until it reaches to the neck of the jug.
- Place an airlock on the secondary fermenter and leave undisturbed in your fermentation area for one month (check periodically to ensure the airlock has not dried out or has otherwise become compromised).
- After one month, check to see that secondary fermentation is complete. Siphon wine off the settled lees. Rack for one to three months more or bottle and store for aging and future use.
- Wines containing rhubarb can sometimes be difficult to clear

and may need a second or even third racking. This wine will benefit from an aging period of 3 to 6 months but can be enjoyed any time after secondary fermentation is complete.

SMALL-BATCH RHUBARB MEAD

MAKES 1 GALLON

Mead is wine made primarily from honey (and yes, you get a recipe for a very good, basic mead here, too). Sometimes fruit will be added to the mead during fermentation for a unique and inviting flavor. Technically when fruit is added to mead the resulting wine is called "melomel," so technically this wine would fall into that category...but mead is probably a more recognizable name for it. But what's in a name? Who cares? This very simple wine brings a lot of good from two worlds, with the subtle taste of rhubarb helping to overcome what can, to some people, be a bit too sweet of a wine and the tartness of the rhubarb balanced by the sweet honey. This small batch is a good introduction to meads and melomels and also provides a mead recipe that won't break the bank for those of you without backyard bees.

Want to play with other fruits or berries for your melomel? Here's an easy substitution guideline: Use four pounds of produce for every gallon batch.

- 4 cups rhubarb
- 4 cups honey (2-pound jar)
- 1 ½ tablespoons lemon juice
- 12 cups water
- 1 packet yeast

- (yeast suggestions: Bread/baker's Active Dry yeast, Premier Classique, EC-1118, Lalvin 71B)

Basic Instructions:

- Wash rhubarb and cut into ¼ to ½ inch pieces.
- Macerate the rhubarb in the honey overnight or up to 48 hours: Place chopped rhubarb in a large bowl and cover with honey (you can use this bowl as your primary fermentation vessel, so make sure it will be large enough and have enough headspace for the next stage). Let sit to allow honey to draw the juices out of the rhubarb. Cover to control fruit flies.
- Add the lemon juice and the water to the bowl. Stir to combine and dissolve the honey.
- Ladle out about 2 cups of the warm must and sugar-water mixture into a small bowl or large measuring cup. Make sure it's not too hot to kill the yeast – between 100°F and 105°F; if hotter, allow to cool before proceeding. Sprinkle the yeast packet evenly over the top of the bowl of must. Rehydrate for 15 minutes, then stir. Let sit an additional 15 minutes until foamy.
- Make sure the bucket of must is at a suitable temperature for yeast introduction (ideally, around 85°F). Pitch the yeast/must mixture into the bowl and stir. Be sure you have a few inches of space at the top of the bowl to prevent overflow from foaming and cap rising once the mead starts to ferment.
- Set the bowl in your designated fermentation area. Do not cover tightly (no lids – primary fermentation requires air); you may choose to cover loosely with a clean linen cloth.
- Let ferment for one week, stirring daily to break up the cap and help keep the honey incorporated.
- After one week, strain off the solids and pour the liquid into a 1-gallon secondary fermenting jug or carboy. Discard rhubarb must. If necessary, top secondary fermenter with water until it reaches to the neck of the jug.
- Place an airlock on the secondary fermenter and leave

undisturbed in your fermentation area for one month (check periodically to ensure the airlock has not dried out or has otherwise become compromised).

- After one month, check to see that secondary fermentation is complete. Siphon wine off the settled lees. Rack for one to three months more or bottle and store for aging and future use. Rhubarb wines can sometimes be difficult to clear and often benefit from an additional racking for a month or two.

- Meads and melomels are often very good at very "young" ages, so do feel free to try your melomel once it has completed fermentation and cleared. A short period of aging can help improve meads as well; three to six months is often recommended.

SMALL-BATCH TRADITIONAL MEAD (HONEY WINE)

MAKES 1 GALLON

Mead is very basic to make, requiring minimal ingredients and preparation. There is no fruit to chop, peel, seed, mush, or macerate in a basic mead; so, if you are looking for an easily-prepared wine to try, give this basic, traditional mead a go. The ratios in this mead make for an almost dry honey wine, not too overpoweringly sweet, and it won't leave you feeling like you've just drank a glass of honey.

- 3 pounds honey
- 1 gallon water
- 1 packet yeast
- (yeast suggestions: Bread/baker's Active Dry yeast, Premier Classique, EC-1118, Lalvin 71B)

Basic Instructions:

- Bring the water just to a simmer. Add the honey to the water and stir to dissolve.
- Let honey and water mixture cool until below 90°F (ideally, around 85°F). Stirring occasionally will help to cool the mixture more quickly.

- Transfer to a large bowl or fermenting bucket/vessel. Be sure that the vessel is large enough to allow two to three inches of headspace so the foamy cap does not overflow the bowl.
- When the must of honey and water is below 90°F, sprinkle the packet of yeast evenly over the top of the honey and water mixture. Let sit to rehydrate for 15 minutes.
- Stir the yeast into the must.
- Set the bowl in your designated fermentation area. Do not cover tightly (no lids – primary fermentation requires air); you may choose to cover loosely with a clean linen cloth or loose plastic wrap.
- Let ferment for about 5 to 7 days, stirring daily to break up the cap, introduce oxygen, and release any trapped carbon dioxide gas.
- After about a week, pour the liquid into a 1-gallon secondary fermenting jug or carboy. If necessary, top secondary fermenter with water until it reaches to the neck of the jug.
- Place an airlock on the secondary fermenter and leave undisturbed in your fermentation area for 4 to 6 weeks (check periodically to ensure the airlock has not dried out or has otherwise become compromised).
- After 4 to 6 weeks, check to see that secondary fermentation is complete. Meads tend to clear more slowly than other types of wine, so the wine may not be completely clear at this point, but you should note signs of stopped fermentation, such as ceased bubbling, some sediment (although without solid ingredients like fruit in the recipe, the lees may be less than you are accustomed to with other wines), and at least the beginning of clearing. If you are not seeing these signs by 6 weeks, or if you are unsure, leave the wine to ferment for another two weeks so that you do not rack or bottle your mead while it is still fermenting.
- Siphon the wine off the settled lees. Rack for one to three months more (recommended) or bottle and store for aging and future use.
- While mead is quite delicious at a young age, it is often not

clear early on, and so a second racking is often necessary before bottling. Once bottled, mead flavors benefit from further aging and development over a three- to six-month period, but mead can be enjoyed any time after secondary fermentation is complete.

MID-BATCH MEAD

MAKES 3 GALLONS

Just a little more honey makes this version just a touch sweeter. If you want it sweeter still, add more honey, up to another couple of pounds. This recipe is otherwise essentially the same as the one-gallon version, provided in a mid-size batch that will be a better volume yield for your time investment.

- 10 pounds honey
- 3 gallons water
- (more later for topping up for secondary fermentation as needed)
- 1 packet yeast
- (yeast suggestions: Bread/baker's Active Dry yeast, Premier Classique, EC-1118, Lalvin 71B)

Basic Instructions:

- Bring the water just to a simmer. Add the honey to the water and stir to dissolve.
- Let honey and water mixture cool until below 90°F (ideally,

around 85°F). Stirring occasionally will help to cool the mixture more quickly.

- Transfer to a fermenting bucket (3- to 5-gallon size). Leave enough room in the bucket to allow 3 or 4 inches of headspace so the foamy cap does not overflow the bowl.
- When the must of honey and water is below 90°F, sprinkle the packet of yeast evenly over the top of the honey and water mixture. Let sit to rehydrate for 15 minutes.
- Stir the yeast into the must.
- Set the bucket in your designated fermentation area. Do not cover tightly (no lids – primary fermentation requires air); you may choose to cover loosely with a clean linen cloth or loose plastic wrap.
- Let ferment for 5 to 7 days, stirring daily to break up the cap, introduce oxygen, and release any trapped carbon dioxide gas.
- After about a week, pour the liquid into a 3-gallon secondary fermenting jug or carboy. If necessary, top secondary fermenter with water until it reaches to the neck of the jug.
- Place an airlock on the secondary fermenter and leave undisturbed in your fermentation area for 4 to 6 weeks (check periodically to ensure the airlock has not dried out or has otherwise become compromised).
- After 4 to 6 weeks, check to see that secondary fermentation is complete. Meads tend to clear more slowly than other types of wine, so the wine may not be completely clear at this point, but you should note signs of stopped fermentation, such as ceased bubbling, some sediment (although without solid ingredients like fruit in the recipe, the lees may be less than you are accustomed to with other wines), and at least the beginning of clearing. If you are not seeing these signs by 6 weeks, or if you are unsure, leave the wine to ferment for another two weeks so that you do not rack or bottle your mead while it is still fermenting.
- Siphon the wine off the settled lees. Rack for one to three months more (recommended) or bottle and store for aging and future use.

- While mead is quite delicious at a young age, it is often not clear early on, and so a second racking is often necessary before bottling. Once bottled, mead flavors benefit from further aging and development over a three- to six-month period, but mead can be enjoyed any time after secondary fermentation is complete.

LARGE-BATCH COUNTRY MEAD

MAKES 5 GALLONS

If you enjoy mead, you'll find there is never enough, and so it's important that we have a large-batch mead recipe, too. This large batch results in a similar wine to the one-gallon batch, nicely balanced and not too sweet. If you'd like to make a very sweet mead, increase honey to between 18 to 20 pounds.

- 16 pounds honey
- 4 gallons water
- (more later for topping up for secondary fermentation)
- 1 packet yeast
- (yeast suggestions: Bread/baker's Active Dry yeast, Premier Classique, EC-1118, Lalvin 71B)

Instructions:

- In a large stock pot, bring about 3 gallons of the water just to a simmer. Add the honey to the water and stir to dissolve.
- Pour the honey and water into a 5-gallon fermentation bucket and add 1 gallon of cool water. Let the honey and water mixture cool further until below 90°F (ideally, around 85°F).

Stirring occasionally will help to cool the mixture more quickly. Be sure to leave about 4 inches of space at the top of the bucket to allow room for the cap to rise as the must ferments.

- When the must of honey and water is below 90°F, sprinkle the packet of yeast evenly over the top of the honey and water mixture. Let sit to rehydrate for 15 minutes.
- Stir the yeast into the must.
- Set the bucket in your designated fermentation area. Do not cover tightly (no lids – primary fermentation requires air); you may choose to cover loosely with a clean linen cloth or loose plastic wrap.
- Let the mead must ferment for 5 to 7 days, stirring daily to break up the cap, introduce oxygen, and release any trapped carbon dioxide gas.
- After about a week, pour the liquid into a 5-gallon secondary fermenting jug or carboy. If necessary, top secondary fermenter with water until it reaches to the neck of the jug.
- Place an airlock on the secondary fermenter and leave undisturbed in your fermentation area for 4 to 6 weeks (check periodically to ensure the airlock has not dried out or has otherwise become compromised).
- After 4 to 6 weeks, check to see that secondary fermentation is complete. Meads tend to clear more slowly than other types of wine, so the wine may not be completely clear at this point, but you should note signs of stopped fermentation, such as ceased bubbling, some sediment (although without solid ingredients like fruit in the recipe, the lees may be less than you are accustomed to with other wines), and at least the beginning of clearing. If you are not seeing these signs by 6 weeks, or if you are unsure, leave the wine to ferment for another two weeks so that you do not rack or bottle your mead while it is still fermenting.
- Siphon the wine off the settled lees. Rack for one to three months more (recommended) or bottle and store for aging and future use.
- While mead is quite delicious at a young age, it is often not

clear early on, and so a second racking is often necessary before bottling. Once bottled, mead flavors benefit from further aging and development over a three- to six-month period, but mead can be enjoyed any time after secondary fermentation is complete.

SPICED METHEGLIN (SPICED HONEY WINE)

MAKES 1 GALLON

Just as a melomel is a mead with a fruit added to it, metheglin is simply a mead fermented with herbs or spices. This particular metheglin recipe uses a variety of spices that you are likely to recognize, and likely to have in your home already, or that otherwise can be readily obtained. Here's a tip – using as many fresh, whole, or chopped versions of the spices as you have available to you (rather than ground) will cause less clouding and help make your mead a little more clear, but ground is fine if whole is difficult to obtain. This recipe is mead stepped up a level, not too sweet but nicely balanced with aromatic spices.

- 2 pounds honey
- 2 large oranges
- 1 gallon water
- (more later for topping up for secondary fermentation as necessary)
- 1 vanilla bean, split open and cut into 1- to 2-inch pieces (if unavailable, substitute 3 teaspoons of good-quality vanilla extract)

- 1 cinnamon stick (if unavailable, substitute ½ teaspoon ground)
- 1 teaspoon fresh ginger, chopped (or ½ teaspoon ground if unavailable)
- ½ teaspoon ground nutmeg
- ½ teaspoon ground allspice (or 1 teaspoon whole if available)
- ¼ teaspoon tea (loose leaf or cut open a tea bag and measure ¼ tsp.)
- 1 packet yeast
- (yeast suggestions: Bread/baker's Active Dry yeast, Premier Classique, EC-1118, Lalvin 71B)

Instructions:

- Bring the water just to a simmer. Add the honey to the water and stir to dissolve.
- Measure out the spices and tea into the bottom a large fermenting bowl, bucket, or vessel (at least 6-quart capacity). If you prefer, you can make a sachet in a small square of cheesecloth.
- Wash the oranges (you do not need to peel) and cut into slices. Place in bottom of fermenting bowl.
- Pour the simmered and dissolved honey and water mixture over the oranges and spices, then stir.
- Let the spiced honey and water mixture cool until below 90°F (ideally, around 85°F). Stirring occasionally will help to cool the mixture more quickly.
- When the must of spiced honey and water is below 90°F, sprinkle the packet of yeast evenly over the top. Let sit to rehydrate for 15 minutes.
- Stir the yeast into the must.
- Set the bowl in your designated fermentation area. Do not cover tightly (no lids – primary fermentation requires air); you may choose to cover loosely with a clean linen cloth or loose plastic wrap.

- Let ferment for 5 to 7 days, stirring daily to break up the cap, introduce oxygen, and release any trapped carbon dioxide gas.
- After about a week, pour the liquid into a 1-gallon secondary fermenting jug or carboy. If necessary, top secondary fermenter with water until it reaches to the neck of the jug.
- Place an airlock on the secondary fermenter and leave undisturbed in your fermentation area for 4 to 6 weeks (check periodically to ensure the airlock has not dried out or has otherwise become compromised).
- After 4 to 6 weeks, check to see that secondary fermentation is complete. Meads tend to clear more slowly than other types of wine, so the wine may not be completely clear at this point, but you should note signs of stopped fermentation, such as ceased bubbling, some sediment (fewer solids in this recipe mean that you can expect the lees to be less than you are accustomed to with other wines), and at least the beginning of clearing. If you are not seeing these signs by 6 weeks, or if you are unsure, leave the wine to ferment for another two weeks so that you do not rack or bottle your mead while it is still fermenting and blow a cap.
- Siphon the wine off the settled lees. Rack for one to three months more (recommended) or bottle and store for aging and future use.
- While mead is quite delicious at a young age, it is often not clear early on, and so a second racking is often necessary before bottling. Once bottled, mead flavors, and spiced metheglins in particular, benefit from further aging and development over a three- to six-month period, but metheglin can be enjoyed any time after secondary fermentation is complete.

APPLE MELOMEL (APPLE HONEY WINE)

MAKES 3 GALLONS

- 12-13 pounds apples
- 10 pounds honey
- 3 gallons water
- (more later for topping up for secondary fermentation as needed)
- 1 packet yeast
- (yeast suggestions: Bread/baker's Active Dry yeast, Premier Classique, EC-1118, Lalvin 71B, K1-V1116)

Instructions:

- Bring 2 gallons of the water just to a simmer (use a minimum 10- to 12- quart capacity stock pot). Add the honey to the water and stir to dissolve. Set aside to cool.
- Wash the apples. Quarter and remove the seeds, then chop. Place chopped apples in the bottom of a 5-gallon fermentation bucket.
- Pour the honey and sugar mixture over the apples and add 1 gallon more of cool water. Be sure there is enough space in the

bucket to allow at least three to four inches of headspace so the foamy cap does not overflow the bucket.

- Ladle out about 2 cups of the warm must and honey-water mixture into a small bowl or large measuring cup. Make sure it's not too hot to kill the yeast – between 100°F and 105°F; if hotter, allow to cool before proceeding. Sprinkle the yeast packet evenly over the top of the bowl of must. Rehydrate for 15 minutes, then stir. Let sit an additional 15 minutes until foamy.
- Let the bucket of must cool until below 90°F (ideally, around 85°F). Stirring occasionally will help to cool the mixture more quickly.
- When the must is below 90°F, pitch the rehydrated yeast mixture in the bucket of must and stir.
- Set the bucket in your designated fermentation area. Do not cover tightly (no lids – primary fermentation requires air); you may choose to cover loosely with a clean linen cloth or loose plastic wrap.
- Let ferment for about 5 to 7 days, stirring daily to break up the cap, introduce oxygen, and release any trapped carbon dioxide gas.
- After about a week, strain out the solids and pour the liquid into a 3-gallon secondary fermenting jug or carboy. If necessary, top secondary fermenter with water until it reaches to the neck of the jug. Discard strained solids.
- Place an airlock on the secondary fermenter and leave undisturbed in your fermentation area for 4 to 6 weeks (check periodically to ensure the airlock has not dried out or has otherwise become compromised).
- After 4 to 6 weeks, check to see that secondary fermentation is complete. Meads and melomels often clear more slowly than other types of wine, so the wine may not be completely clear at this point, but you should note signs of stopped fermentation such as ceased bubbling, sediment, and at least the beginning of clearing. If you are not seeing these signs by 6 weeks, or if you are unsure, leave the wine to ferment for another two

weeks so that you do not rack or bottle your melomel while it is still fermenting.

- Siphon the wine off the settled lees. Rack for one to three months more (recommended) or bottle and store for aging and future use.
- Melomels can be enjoyed at a young age but often are not clear early on, and so a second racking is often necessary before bottling. Once bottled, melomel flavors benefit from further aging and development over a three- to six-month period, but the wine can be enjoyed any time after secondary fermentation is complete.

APPLE WINE

MAKE 5 GALLONS

Apple wine recipes run the gamut from very dry to very sweet, with very sweet often being what you find commercially. This recipe should land you somewhere towards the dry to semi-sweet end of the spectrum. The types of apples you choose will have some influence since the natural sugar content of apples can vary from variety to variety. Many winemakers choose a variety mix, which helps with balance, but you should feel free to use what is available to you. In fact, sweeter eating apples like "delicious" varieties are not the best option, and something more like a Macintosh or even crabapples are preferred. Myself, I go for the less expensive but still good quality seconds or drops from the local orchard that maybe have a blemish or two to cut out, but that are sold fairly cheaply in bulk (and that are always better than old shipped and battered grocery store apples!).

- 35 pounds apples
- 10 pounds sugar
- 4 gallons water, divided
- (more later for topping up for secondary fermentation)
- 1 packet yeast

- (yeast suggestions: Bread/baker's Active Dry yeast, Premier Classique, Premier Blanc, K1-V1116, EC-1118)

Instructions:

- Wash apples.
- Simmer the 10 pounds of sugar in 2 gallons of the water until dissolved. Set aside and let cool as you prepare the must.
- Remove apple stems and seeds and chop into 1- to 2- inch pieces (or better yet, use a fruit press if you have one and reserve both the juice and the pulp).
- Place the must of chopped or crushed apples into a clean fermenting bucket, five gallons or larger.
- Add the sugar and water mixture and stir through.
- Ladle out about 2 cups of the warm must and sugar water mixture into a small bowl or large measuring cup. Make sure it's not too hot to kill the yeast – between 100°F and 105°F; if hotter, allow to cool before proceeding. Sprinkle the yeast packet evenly over the top of the bowl of must. Rehydrate for 15 minutes, then stir. Let sit an additional 15 minutes until foamy.
- Add enough of the remaining water to the bucket of must to top up the volume. Leave about 4-5 inches at the top of the bucket to allow the cap space to rise without overflowing the bucket.
- Make sure the bucket of must is not too hot (ideally, around 85°F — you can add some cool water to help cool it down if necessary and space allows). Pitch the yeast/must mixture into the bucket of must and stir.
- Set the bucket in your designated fermentation area. Do not cover tightly (no lids – primary fermentation requires air); you may choose to cover loosely with a clean linen cloth.
- Let ferment for one week, stirring daily to break up the cap.
- After one week, strain off the solids and pour the liquid into a 5-gallon secondary fermenting jug or carboy. Discard must.

Top the secondary fermenter with water until it reaches to the neck of the jug.

- Place an airlock on the secondary fermenter and leave undisturbed in your fermentation area for one month (check periodically to ensure the airlock has not dried out or has otherwise become compromised).
- After one month, check to see that secondary fermentation is complete. Siphon wine off the settled lees. Rack for one to three months more or bottle and store for aging and future use.
- Lighter wines like apple wines don't need as long to age as other wines. Apple wine can benefit from an aging period of three to six months, but is also good at a young age and may be enjoyed any time after primary fermentation is complete.

PEAR WINE

Pear wine is pretty similar to apple wine in preparation and in result. Depending on your variety of fruit, you may even have a hard time telling the difference. For a little more depth, I've seen some recipes where brown sugar will be cut into the sugar requirement (at a rate of about 2 pounds for every 3 pounds of white sugar) – something to think about if you like to play!

- 25 pounds pears
- 10 pounds sugar
- 4 gallons water, divided
- (more later for topping up for secondary fermentation)
- 1 packet yeast
- (yeast suggestions: Bread/baker's Active Dry yeast, Premier Classique, Premier Blanc, K1-V1116, EC-1118)

Instructions:

- Wash and drain pears.
- Remove pear stems and seeds and chop into 1- to 2- inch

pieces (or better yet, use a fruit press if you have one and reserve both the juice and the pulp).

- Place the must of chopped or crushed pears into a clean fermenting bucket, five gallons or larger.
- Add the sugar and water mixture and stir through.
- Ladle out about 2 cups of the warm must and sugar-water mixture into a small bowl or large measuring cup. Make sure it's not too hot to kill the yeast – between 100°F and 105°F; if hotter, allow to cool before proceeding. Sprinkle the yeast packet evenly over the top of the bowl of must. Rehydrate for 15 minutes, then stir. Let sit an additional 15 minutes until foamy.
- Add enough of the remaining water to the bucket of must to top up the volume. Leave about 4-5 inches at the top of the bucket to allow the cap space to rise without overflowing the bucket.
- Make sure the bucket of must is not too hot (ideally, around 85°F — you can add some cool water to help cool it down if necessary and space allows). Pitch the yeast/must mixture into the bucket of must and stir.
- Set the bucket in your designated fermentation area. Do not cover tightly (no lids – primary fermentation requires air); you may choose to cover loosely with a clean linen cloth.
- Let ferment for one week, stirring daily to break up the cap.
- After one week, strain off the solids and pour the liquid into a 5-gallon secondary fermenting jug or carboy. Discard must. Top the secondary fermenter with water until it reaches to the neck of the jug.
- Place an airlock on the secondary fermenter and leave undisturbed in your fermentation area for one month (check periodically to ensure the airlock has not dried out or has otherwise become compromised).
- After one month, check to see that secondary fermentation is complete. Siphon wine off the settled lees. Rack for one to three months more or bottle and store for aging and future use.

- Like apple wine, pear wines don't need as long to age as other wines. Pear wine will benefit from a three- to six-month aging period, but you may enjoy drinking it right away after secondary fermentation is complete, or start enjoying it within a month or two.

SUMMER PEACH WINE

MAKES 5 GALLONS

Peach...one of those quintessential tastes of summer. This is a wine you will enjoy on a sunny evening; a little sunshine in a glass. It is also a nicely balanced light to white wine with a little body that you will enjoy having at any time of the year, the taste of reminiscence. A larger fruit that adds up quickly, it's not too hard to obtain peaches in quantity and the fruit works up with ease. A late-afternoon summer porch project to enjoy while listening to some favorite tunes or a good audiobook!

- 20-25 pounds peaches
- 10 pounds sugar
- 4 gallons water, divided
- (more later for topping up for secondary fermentation)
- 1 packet yeast
- (yeast suggestions: Bread/baker's Active Dry yeast, Premier Classique, Premier Blanc, K1-V1116, EC-1118)

Instructions:

- Wash and drain peaches.

- Simmer the 10 pounds of sugar in 2 gallons of the water until dissolved. Set aside and let cool as you prepare the must.
- Cut peaches into halves, remove the pits, and then chop or cut peaches into 2-inch pieces (or press if you have a fruit press; reserve both juice and pulp for must).
- Place the must of crushed peaches into a clean fermenting bucket, five gallons or larger.
- Add the sugar-water mixture and stir through.
- Ladle out about 2 cups of the warm must and sugar-water mixture into a small bowl or large measuring cup. Make sure it's not too hot to kill the yeast – between 100°F and 105°F; if hotter, allow to cool before proceeding. Sprinkle the yeast packet evenly over the top of the bowl of must. Rehydrate for 15 minutes, then stir. Let sit an additional 15 minutes until foamy.
- Add enough of the remaining 3 gallons of water to the bucket of must to top up the volume. Leave about 4-5 inches at the top of the bucket to allow the cap space to rise without overflowing the bucket.
- Make sure the bucket of must is not too hot (ideally, around 85°F – you can add some cool water to help cool it down if necessary and if space allows). Pitch the yeast/must mixture into the bucket of must and stir.
- Set the bucket in your designated fermentation area. Do not cover tightly (no lids – primary fermentation requires air); you may choose to cover loosely with a clean linen cloth.
- Let ferment for one week, stirring daily to break up the cap.
- After one week, strain off the solids and pour the liquid into a 5-gallon secondary fermenting jug or carboy. Discard fruit must. Top secondary fermenter with water until it reaches to the neck of the jug.
- Place an airlock on the secondary fermenter and leave undisturbed in your fermentation area for one month (check periodically to ensure the airlock has not dried out or has otherwise become compromised).
- After one month, check to see that secondary fermentation is

complete. Siphon wine off the settled lees. Rack for one to three months more or bottle and store for aging and future use.

- Peach wine is very good at almost any point after secondary fermentation is complete, so you may drink it young or you may choose to let it age for a few months.

PERFECTLY PLUM WINE

MAKES 3 GALLONS

Sweeter and heavier than many fruit wines, plum wine is best known as a Japanese-inspired sipping wine. Traditional versions can be very sweet and very heavy, often leaning towards a liqueur or cordial, so it benefits to start making your own plum wine at home and getting that body and sweetness just to your liking. You'll note the sugar to fruit ratio in this wine is nearly equal, so for something a little less sweet, start by cutting back a bit on the sugar.

- 7-8 pounds plums
- 6 pounds sugar
- 3 gallons water, divided
- (more later for topping up for secondary fermentation)
- 1 packet yeast
- (yeast suggestions: Bread/baker's Active Dry yeast, Premier Classique, EC-1118)

Instructions:

- Wash and drain plums.

- Simmer the 6 pounds of sugar in 1 ½ gallons of the water until dissolved. Set aside and let cool as you prepare the must.
- Cut plums in half and remove pits. Cut into 1- to 2-inch pieces. Mash lightly with a masher.
- Place must of crushed plums into a clean fermenting bucket, (five-gallon size is good).
- Add the sugar and water mixture and stir through.
- Ladle out about 2 cups of the warm must and sugar-water mixture into a small bowl or large measuring cup. Make sure it's not too hot to kill the yeast – between 100°F and 105°F; if hotter, allow to cool before proceeding. Sprinkle the yeast packet evenly over the top of the bowl of must. Rehydrate for 15 minutes, then stir. Let sit an additional 15 minutes until foamy.
- Add the remaining 1 ½ gallons of water, making sure there is room left in the bucket for the cap to rise without overflowing the bucket (at least 4-5 inches of space; more is fine).
- Make sure the bucket of must is not too hot (ideally, around 85°F — you can add some cool water to help cool it down if necessary but not more than 3 gallons total for the batch). Pitch the yeast/must mixture into the bucket of must and stir.
- Set the bucket in your designated fermentation area. Do not cover tightly (no lids – primary fermentation requires air); you may choose to cover loosely with a clean linen cloth.
- Let ferment for one week, stirring daily to break up the cap.
- After one week, strain off the solids and pour the liquid into a 3-gallon secondary fermenting jug or carboy. Discard must. Top the secondary fermenter with water until it reaches to the neck of the jug.
- Place an airlock on the secondary fermenter and leave undisturbed in your fermentation area for one month (check periodically to ensure the airlock has not dried out or has otherwise become compromised).
- After one month, check to see that secondary fermentation is complete. Siphon wine off the settled lees. Rack for one to three months more or bottle and store for aging and future use.

- Though plum wine is safe to drink any time after secondary fermentation is complete, young plum wine can often come off as harsh or astringent, and so plum wine benefits from a longer aging period of six to twelve months. Try it at different stages and note when you think your plum wine became most enjoyable.

CHERRY WINE

MAKES 3 GALLONS

One thing said about cherry wine is that it is a treat, but you don't want to skimp on the cherries. People use a variety of cherries for their cherry wines, including everything from tiny chokecherries (a true country tradition for those who know it) to commercial Bing cherries and every mixture in between. Cherries tend to be low in acid and so a couple of lemons thrown into the must can help to balance and protect the wine over time.

- 12 pounds fruit
- 6 pounds sugar
- 2 whole lemons
- 3 gallons water, divided
- (more later for topping up for secondary fermentation)
- 1 packet yeast
- (yeast suggestions: Bread/baker's Active Dry yeast, Premier Classique)

Instructions:

- Wash and destem cherries and de-pit as much as possible (a few pits won't hurt but be sure to discard cracked or broken pits).

- Wash the lemons and cut into slices.
- Simmer the 6 pounds of sugar in 1 ½ gallons of the water until dissolved. Set aside and let cool as you prepare the must.
- Crush the cherries or mash with a masher and release as much juice as possible. Work in batches so that all fruits or berries are equally destroyed.
- Place the must of crushed cherries and the sliced lemons into a clean fermenting bucket, (5-gallon size is good).
- Add the sugar and water mixture and stir through.
- Ladle out about 2 cups of the warm must and sugar-water mixture into a small bowl or large measuring cup. Make sure it's not too hot to kill the yeast – between 100°F and 105°F; if hotter, allow to cool before proceeding. Sprinkle the yeast packet evenly over the top of the bowl of must. Rehydrate for 15 minutes, then stir. Let sit an additional 15 minutes until foamy.
- Add the remaining 1 ½ gallons of water, making sure there is room left in the bucket for the cap to rise without overflowing the bucket (at least 4-5 inches of space; more is fine).
- Make sure the bucket of must is not too hot (ideally, around 85°F — you can add some cool water to help cool it down if necessary and volume allows). Pitch the yeast/must mixture into the bucket of must and stir.
- Set the bucket in your designated fermentation area. Do not cover tightly (no lids – primary fermentation requires air); you may choose to cover loosely with a clean linen cloth.
- Let ferment for one week, stirring daily to break up the cap.
- After one week, strain off the solids and pour the liquid into a 3-gallon secondary fermenting jug or carboy. Discard must. Top secondary fermenter with water until it reaches to the neck of the jug.
- Place an airlock on the secondary fermenter and leave undisturbed in your fermentation area for one month (check

periodically to ensure the airlock has not dried out or has otherwise become compromised).

- After one month, check to see that secondary fermentation is complete. Siphon the wine off the settled lees. Rack for one to three months more or bottle and store for aging and future use.
- Cherry wine is generally thought to require a minimum of six months to age. You may drink the wine any time after secondary fermentation has completed but aging between six and twelve months is likely to improve it a great deal.

CRANBERRY WINE

MAKES 5 GALLONS

My experience playing with cranberry wine recipes has been that it is difficult to achieve a good cranberry flavor with just cranberries alone. A little experimentation has brought me to this recipe, a mixture of cranberry and grape supported with cranberry juice. This delivers a light yet flavorful batch of wine that is perfect for holiday pairing.

- 5 pounds fresh cranberries
- 10 pounds grapes
- 4, 64-ounce bottles (2 gallons) 100% cranberry juice (no sugar added)
- 6 pounds sugar
- 2 gallons water, divided
- (more later for topping up for secondary fermentation)
- 1 packet yeast
- (yeast suggestions: Bread/baker's Active Dry yeast, Premier Classique, EC-1118)

Instructions:

- Wash and destem fruit.

- Simmer the 6 pounds of sugar in 1 gallon of the water until dissolved. Set aside and let cool as you prepare the must.
- Lightly chop the cranberries.
- Crush grapes and release as much juice as possible. Work in batches so that all grapes are equally destroyed.
- Place the chopped berries and the crushed grapes into a clean fermenting bucket, five gallons or larger.
- Add the sugar and water mixture and stir through. Add the cranberry juice and stir.
- Ladle out about 2 cups of the warm must and juice/sugar-water mixture into a small bowl or large measuring cup. Make sure it's not too hot to kill the yeast – between 100°F and 105°F; if hotter, allow to cool before proceeding. Sprinkle the yeast packet evenly over the top of the bowl of must. Rehydrate for 15 minutes, then stir. Let sit an additional 15 minutes until foamy.
- Add enough of the remaining 2 gallons of water to the bucket of must to top up the volume. Leave about 4-5 inches at the top of the bucket to allow the cap space to rise without overflowing the bucket.
- Make sure the bucket of must is not too hot (ideally, around 85°F — you can add some cool water to help cool it down if necessary). Pitch the yeast/must mixture into the bucket of must and stir.
- Set the bucket in your designated fermentation area. Do not cover tightly (no lids – primary fermentation requires air); you may choose to cover loosely with a clean linen cloth.
- Let ferment for one week, stirring daily to break up the cap.
- After one week, strain off the solids and pour the liquid into a 5-gallon secondary fermenting jug or carboy. Discard the strained must. Top secondary fermenter with water until it reaches to the neck of the jug.
- Place an airlock on the secondary fermenter and leave undisturbed in your fermentation area for one month (check periodically to ensure the airlock has not dried out or has otherwise become compromised).

- After one month, check to see that secondary fermentation is complete. Siphon the wine off the settled lees. Rack for one to three months more or bottle and store for aging and future use.
- While this cranberry wine will benefit from a moderate aging period of about 6 months, it can also be enjoyed "young", at any time after secondary fermentation is complete.

EARTH'S ESSENCE ELDERBERRY WINE

MAKES 5 GALLONS

If you're not familiar with elderberries, get acquainted. Elderberries grow wild throughout North America. They have a deep, earthy flavor that is really unlike any other berry. They are touted for immune support and high antioxidant power, to name just a couple benefits. What's even better is that they make DELICIOUS wine! Particularly if you enjoy deeper and dryer red wines, you will fall in love with home-made elderberry wine. Elderberry wine is best made from fresh or fresh-frozen berries. They can be difficult to obtain from growers because their fresh and fresh/frozen crop sells out fast, but there are options for making the wine with a vintner's juice or rehydrated berries, too, which comes in a fair second place.

Raw elderberries and elderberry stems contain irritating toxins. Cooking and fermenting breaks down these elements and makes elderberries safe to eat and drink. You won't likely remove every stem from your berries in the prep process, but remove what you reasonably can and do not eat stems or raw elderberries. It is also advisable to wear gloves while crushing berries – they can get quite irritatingly sticky and staining!

- 15-18 pounds elderberries
- 12 pounds sugar (10 for an even drier wine)

- 2 teaspoons tea (optional)
- 4 gallons water, divided
- (more later for topping up for secondary fermentation)
- 1 packet yeast
- (yeast suggestions: Bread/baker's Active Dry yeast, Premier Classique, Premier Rouge)

Instructions:

- Wash elderberries and remove from stems. Ripe elderberries will easily come off stems by gently rolling and pulling them with your fingers. Another trick of the trade is to use a fork to "rake" them off the stems.
- Simmer the 12 pounds of sugar in 2 gallons of the water until dissolved. Set aside and let cool as you prepare the must.
- Crush the berries and release as much juice as possible. Work in batches so that all fruits or berries are equally destroyed. If you have a fruit press available, this works well with elderberries in a fine-mesh bag.
- Place the must of crushed fruit into a clean fermenting bucket, five gallons or larger. Add tea if using.
- Add the sugar and water mixture and stir through.
- Ladle out about 2 cups of the warm must and sugar-water mixture into a small bowl or large measuring cup. Make sure it's not too hot to kill the yeast – between 100°F and 105°F; if hotter, allow to cool before proceeding. Sprinkle the yeast packet evenly over the top of the bowl of must. Rehydrate for 15 minutes, then stir. Let sit an additional 15 minutes until foamy.
- Add enough of the remaining 2 gallons of water to the bucket of must to top up the volume. Leave about 4-5 inches at the top of the bucket to allow the cap space to rise without overflowing the bucket.
- Make sure the bucket of must is not too hot (ideally, around 85°F — you can add some cool water to help cool it down if

necessary). Pitch the yeast/must mixture into the bucket of must and stir.

- Set the bucket in your designated fermentation area. Do not cover tightly (no lids – primary fermentation requires air); you may choose to cover loosely with a clean linen cloth.
- Let ferment for one week, stirring daily to break up the cap.
- After one week, strain off the solids and pour the liquid into a 5-gallon secondary fermenting jug or carboy. Discard must. Top secondary fermenter with water until it reaches to the neck of the jug.
- Place an airlock on the secondary fermenter and leave undisturbed in your fermentation area for one month (check periodically to ensure the airlock has not dried out or has otherwise become compromised).
- After one month, check to see that secondary fermentation is complete. Siphon wine off the settled lees. Rack for one to three months more or bottle and store for aging and future use.
- Young elderberry wine tends to have a harsh mouth-feel, which the addition of the tea can help mitigate. While safe to consumer early on after secondary fermentation has completed, an aging period of at least 6 months is most commonly recommended, with many saying they never drink their elderberry wine before 12 months. (We drink our elderberry anywhere from 3 months on, and while it does mellow and the harshness softens with age, few of the bottles ever make 12 months in our home. It's our household's absolute fan-favorite, and the requested wine of friends in the know!)

VINTNER'S JUICE ELDERBERRY WINE

MAKES 5 GALLONS

I'll be honest. This recipe for elderberry wine is not as good as the one that precedes it. But, as mentioned, elderberries can be difficult to obtain, especially fresh, unless you have identified sources and have a plan for foraging. And even then, you have to beat the birds to them (and those birds only give you a couple of days! Do not wait once ripe!). And so, sometimes your best option is to make a batch of elderberry wine from the resources you have available to you, and the next-best resource is usually a prepared vintner's wine-making juice. With a little experimentation I've tweaked the basic recipe to round out the flavors, and the result is a pretty good elderberry wine that anyone can make with a little online ordering, and which serves a decent substitute when you run out of elderberry wine in January and have to get through to August to harvest more.

- 1, 96 ounce can Elderberry Wine Base (elderberry vintner's juice)
- 6 cans (4 ½ gallons) water
- 12 pounds sugar
- 2 lemons
- 2 oranges

- 1 pound dried elderberries (about 4 cups; optional, but helps add elderberry flavor)
- 1 packet yeast
- (yeast suggestions: Bread/baker's Active Dry yeast, Premier Classique, Premier Rouge)

Instructions:

- Simmer the 12 pounds of sugar in 2 gallons of the water until dissolved.
- Pour the wine base (elderberry juice) into the primary fermenting bucket (5-gallon bucket). Pour the sugar-water mixture into the bucket. Stir.
- Add enough cool water to the bucket to total about 4 gallons, but leave at least 5 inches of headspace in the bucket for the addition of other ingredients and rising cap during fermentation.
- When the juice has cooled to below 85°F, sprinkle the packet of yeast over the top of the juice and water mixture and let sit to rehydrate as you prepare additional ingredients.
- Wash the outsides of the lemons and oranges and cut into slices. Dried elderberries are ready to use out of the bag.
- When yeast has rehydrated (about 15 minutes), stir into the juice to incorporate.
- Add the sliced citrus and the dried elderberries. Stir.
- Set the bucket in your designated fermentation area. Do not cover tightly (no lids – primary fermentation requires air); you may choose to cover loosely with a clean linen cloth.
- Let ferment for one week, stirring daily to break up the cap.
- After one week, strain off the solids and pour the liquid into a 5-gallon secondary fermenting jug or carboy. Discard the fruit must. Top the secondary fermenter with water until it reaches to the neck of the jug.
- Place an airlock on the secondary fermenter and leave undisturbed in your fermentation area for one month (check

periodically to ensure the airlock has not dried out or has otherwise become compromised).

- After one month, check to see that secondary fermentation is complete. Siphon the wine off the settled lees. Rack for one to three months more or bottle and store for aging and future use.
- Elderberry wine is safe to drink any time after secondary fermentation is complete, but benefits from an aging period of six months or more.

ELDERFLOWER WINE

MAKES 1 GALLON

Elderflower is a delicate flavor which is delightful in a wine when done right. The result is a subtly floral white wine, delicious served cool or cold on a warm evening (and also enjoyable as a white wine spritzer). If either wild or cultivated elderberries are available to you, start looking in June when the large white umbels of flowers start to bloom. It is recommended to pick the umbels in the morning when the fragrance is freshest and strongest. I often take my harvest of elder-flowers from roadside bushes that are likely to be mowed before the berries can ripen anyway, or otherwise from bushes that could benefit from a little blossom-pruning to increase the size of the remaining berries. Late-blooming umbels are also good choices for elderflower harvest, because they are unlikely to ripen with the rest of the bush, and so they won't be much use in the elderberry harvest. Here's one final tip – note the location of the bushes you find when hunting for elderflowers; elderberries are easiest to spot when they are in bloom, and you might not remember where to find them all later when you want to go back for those berries!

Note: If fresh elderflowers are not available to you, this recipe can also be prepared using dried elderflowers, which you can purchase in bulk online. Use half as much dehydrated flowers as fresh.

- 4 to 6 cups fresh elderflowers (about 24 umbels; if using dried flowers, 2 to 3 cups)
- 2 ½ pounds sugar
- 1 gallon water
- 2 lemons
- ½ teaspoon tea
- 1 packet yeast
- (yeast suggestions: Bread/baker's Active Dry yeast, Premier Classique, Premier Blanc, EC-1118)

Basic Instructions:

- Shake elderflower blossoms to dislodge any insects and dirt and rinse under running water.
- Snip or pull elderflowers from the stems (as much as possible – some small stems will be okay).
- Wash lemons and cut into slices (or squeeze juice and discard fruit).
- Place the stripped elderflowers, the tea, and the lemons in a large bowl, large enough for primary fermentation.
- Simmer the 2 ½ pounds of sugar in 4 quarts of water until dissolved. Pour hot (carefully!) over the elderflowers and added ingredients.
- Cover lightly with plastic wrap and let sit overnight or for up to 24 hours so that flowers can steep.
- The next day, warm about 2 cups of the elderflower must to around 80-85°F. Sprinkle the packet of yeast over the top and let rehydrate for 15 minutes, then stir and let sit an additional 15 minutes until foamy.
- Add the proofed yeast to the elderflower must and stir through.
- Set the bowl in your designated fermentation area. Do not cover tightly (no lids – primary fermentation requires air); you may choose to cover loosely with a clean linen cloth.
- Let ferment for one week, stirring daily to break up the cap and keep the flowers in the liquid.

- After one week, strain off solids and pour the liquid into a 1-gallon secondary fermenting jug or carboy. Discard the flower/fruit must. Top secondary fermenter with water until it reaches to the neck of the jug.
- Place an airlock on the secondary fermenter and leave undisturbed in your fermentation area for one month (check periodically to ensure the airlock has not dried out or has otherwise become compromised).
- After one month, check to see that secondary fermentation is complete. Siphon the wine off the settled lees. Rack for one to three months more or bottle and store for aging and future use.
- Though you may drink elderflower wine at any time after secondary fermentation is complete, it will benefit from an aging period of six to twelve months.

BEET COUNTRY WINE (BEETROOT WINE)

MAKES 1 GALLON

It's true – wine can be made from virtually any fruit *or vegetable*. And sometimes the results are quite surprising – like this recipe for simple country Beet Wine. Oddly refreshing and earthy, if you're up for some fun and experimentation, give this recipe a try. You might even find you really like it!

- 3 to 4 pounds beets
- 3 pounds sugar
- 1 gallon water, divided
- 4 to 6 whole cloves (optional)
- 1-inch piece fresh ginger (chopped; optional)
- 1 packet yeast
- (yeast suggestions: Bread/baker's Active Dry yeast, Premier Classique)

Instructions:

- Wash and scrub the beets to remove all dirt. Peeling is usually recommended, but if you wash and scrub well with steel wool you will often find this is not necessary.

- Cut the beets into quarters and place in a pan with about 2 quarts of water (more if needed to cover the beets). Bring to a boil and boil until tender (probably a little softer than you would normally cook the beets for eating).
- Pour the hot cooking liquid into a large (heatproof) bowl. Add the sugar and stir (carefully but well) until the sugar dissolves. Let sit to cool.
- Mash the beets with a potato masher and then add them to the bowl of sugar and beet juice. If using ginger and spices, add them now.
- Add 2 quarts of cold water and stir.
- Make sure the must is not too hot to kill the yeast – ideally, around 85°F; if hotter, allow to cool before proceeding.
- Sprinkle the yeast packet evenly over the top of the bowl of must. Rehydrate for 15 minutes, then stir.
- Set the bowl in your designated fermentation area. Do not cover tightly (no lids – primary fermentation requires air); you may choose to cover loosely with a clean linen cloth.
- Let ferment for one week, stirring daily to break up the cap.
- After one week, strain off the solids and pour the liquid into a 1-gallon secondary fermenting jug or carboy. Discard the must. Top the secondary fermenter with water until it reaches to the neck of the jug.
- Place an airlock on the secondary fermenter and leave undisturbed in your fermentation area for one month (check periodically to ensure the airlock has not dried out or has otherwise become compromised).
- After one month, check to see that secondary fermentation is complete. Siphon the wine off the settled lees. Rack for one to three months more or bottle and store for aging and future use.
- As with any wine, beet wine may be enjoyed at any time after secondary fermentation is complete, but it should improve with an aging period of 3 to 6 months or more.

TOMATO COUNTRY WINE

MAKES 3 GALLONS

Tomato wine was probably my first introduction to vegetable wines. Once I thought about it, it made sense – because as anyone who has ever grown tomatoes comes to know, at some time you will have far too many tomatoes, and there is only so much saucing and canning a body can do. And so, it seems quite logical that someone, somewhere gave tomato wine a try. And many of those people swear by it! It's been called fruity and spicy, and sherry-like. Tomato wine is most often compared to a basic white wine and the recommendation is to serve it chilled. One thing, though – almost every recipe you come across recommends aging tomato wine for one to two *years*.

- 12 pounds tomatoes
- 6 pounds sugar
- 3 gallons water, divided
- (more later for topping up for secondary fermentation)
- 1 packet yeast
- (yeast suggestions: Bread/baker's Active Dry yeast, Premier Classique, EC-1118)

Instructions:

- Wash and drain tomatoes.
- Simmer the 6 pounds of sugar in 1 ½ gallons of the water until dissolved. Set aside and let cool as you prepare the must.
- Cut the core from the tomatoes and cut or chop into pieces about 2 inches in size.
- Working in batches, crush or mash the tomato chunks with a kitchen masher. Add batches to clean fermenting bucket (five-gallon size is good).
- Add the sugar and water mixture and stir through.
- Ladle out about 2 cups of the warm must and sugar-water mixture into a small bowl or large measuring cup. Make sure it's not too hot to kill the yeast – between 100°F and 105°F; if hotter, allow to cool before proceeding. Sprinkle the yeast packet evenly over the top of the bowl of must. Rehydrate for 15 minutes, then stir. Let sit an additional 15 minutes until foamy.
- Add the remaining 1 ½ gallons of water, making sure there is room left in the bucket for the cap to rise without overflowing the bucket (at least 4-5 inches of space; more is fine).
- Make sure the bucket of must is not too hot (ideally, around 85°F — you can add some cool water to help cool it down if necessary and space allows). Pitch the yeast/must mixture into the bucket of must and stir.
- Set the bucket in your designated fermentation area. Do not cover tightly (no lids – primary fermentation requires air); you may choose to cover loosely with a clean linen cloth.
- Let ferment for one week, stirring daily to break up the cap.
- After one week, strain off the solids and pour the liquid into a 3-gallon secondary fermenting jug or carboy. Discard must. Top secondary fermenter with water until it reaches to the neck of the jug.
- Place an airlock on the secondary fermenter and leave undisturbed in your fermentation area for one month (check

periodically to ensure the airlock has not dried out or has otherwise become compromised).

- After one month, check to see that secondary fermentation is complete. Siphon the wine off the settled lees. Rack for one to three months more or bottle and store for aging and future use. You may choose to rack the tomato wine a third time before bottling after more lees have settled out.

- It is recommended that tomato wine undergo a long aging period of one to two years. However, you may drink your tomato wine any time after secondary fermentation is complete.

EASY GROCERY-STORE GRAPE WINE

MAKES 1 GALLON

As said earlier on, wine can even be made from everyday grocery store items. Here's a simple and basic recipe to prove the point.

- 3 cans (11.5/12 ounce size) frozen grape juice concentrate
- 6 cans warm water (using the same can – about 80°F)
- ½ cup sugar
- 1 packet yeast
- (yeast suggestion: Bread/baker's Active Dry yeast)

Instructions:

- Thaw and bring juice concentrate to room temperature.
- In a large bowl, mix together the grape juice concentrate and the cans of water.
- Stir in the sugar until it completely dissolves.
- Sprinkle the yeast over the surface of the juice and let rehydrate for 15 minutes, then stir it into the juice.
- Ferment juice in designated area for several days, and then pour it into a one-gallon jug for secondary fermentation.

- Fix jug with an airlock and ferment for about 4 weeks more.
- Once fermentation has stopped, siphon or strain off any sediment. Bottle and enjoy.

BASICALLY BASIC VINTNER'S JUICE WINE RECIPE

MAKES 5 GALLONS

Here is a run-down of a very basic recipe using wine bases or vintner's juices in combination with the cheap-and-easy wine-making process. If you are purchasing a wine "kit" it is sure to come with its own set of instructions, and cans typically have some guidance and instructions printed on them as well, but they may also include additives and ingredients you won't care to use. Further, there are a lot of places to buy juices for making wine online without buying a complete kit, and so it never hurts to have a basic set of instructions handy, just-in-case. One last note worth the mention – if you ever find yourself with extra homemade fruit juice that you've canned or frozen for future projects, this recipe works there, too.

- 1, 96 ounce can Wine Base (vintner's juice)
- 6 cans (4 ½ gallons) water
- 12 pounds sugar
- Juice of 2 lemons or ¼ cup lemon juice
- Optional: Additional fresh or dried fruit for flavor if desired (1 to 5 pounds)
- Optional: ½ pound raisins (acts as yeast nutrient and improves

"mouth feel"; white raisins may be used if preferred and may be preferable in lighter juices)
- 1 packet yeast
- (yeast suggestions: Bread/baker's Active Dry Yeast, Premier Classique, Premier Rouge)

Instructions:

- Simmer the 12 pounds of sugar in 2 gallons of the water until dissolved.
- Pour the wine base into the primary fermenting bucket (use at least a 5-gallon bucket). Pour the sugar-water mixture into the bucket. Stir.
- Add lemon juice.
- Add (optional) raisins and fresh or dried fruit if using.
- Add enough cool water to the bucket to total about 4 gallons, but leave at least 5 inches of headspace in the bucket to allow the cap space to rise without overflowing the bucket during fermentation.
- When the juice has cooled to below 85°F, sprinkle the packet of yeast over the top of the juice and water mixture and let sit to rehydrate.
- When yeast has rehydrated (about 15 minutes), stir into the juice to incorporate.
- Set the bucket in your designated fermentation area. Do not cover tightly (no lids – primary fermentation requires air); you may choose to cover loosely with a clean linen cloth.
- Ferment for one week, stirring daily to break up the cap and de-gas.
- After one week, strain off the solids (if you included raisins or fruit) and pour the liquid into a 5-gallon secondary fermenting jug or carboy. Discard any solids. Top the secondary fermenter with water until it reaches to the neck of the jug.
- Place an airlock on the secondary fermenter and leave undisturbed in your fermentation area for one month (check

periodically to ensure that the airlock has not dried out or has otherwise become compromised).

- After one month, check to see that secondary fermentation is complete. Siphon the wine off the settled lees. Rack for one to three months more or bottle and store for aging and future use.
- Recommended aging for specific wines will vary depending on the juice base. Generally speaking, though, wines made from wine bases can be enjoyed more towards the younger side of aging. Lighter and white wines require less aging and are good as young as three to six months old. Darker, heavier red juices usually have recommended aging periods of six to twelve months. At any rate, even young wines are pretty good and can be enjoyed any time after secondary fermentation is complete.

MULLED WINE

Think the fun is over with the winemaking? That is where the fun just begins!

Of course, drinking those fabulous fermented fruits of your labor is divine, but there could come some days and special occasions that have you looking toward something just a little different to do with your wine. (And let's be honest; there may also be wines that are just a little sub-par but that could really be helped and made more useful with a little embellishment. Hey – we've all been there!)

Warm mulled wine is just the ticket for times such as these when the weather turns cold. It is a traditional holiday drink and perfect for frosty get-togethers throughout the colder parts of the year. And there's almost nothing easier to make!

Here is a simple, basic, delicious recipe for mulled wine. It is best suited to reds, usually the darker the better. In our home (can you guess?) we think elderberry is the perfect wine for mulling. Blackberry, apple, or pear would be excellent, too, or possibly a mix of wines that strikes your fancy.

- One 750 ml bottle or about 1 quart red wine

- 1 orange, washed, unpeeled, sliced
- 10 whole cloves
- 3 cinnamon sticks
- 3 whole star anise
- ¼ cup honey (or sugar, more or less to taste)
- ¼ cup brandy (optional)

For garnish, optional:

- orange slices, cut into halves or quarters
- cinnamon sticks
- whole star anise

On the stovetop:

Combine all ingredients except the garnishes in a large pot and heat over medium-high heat until wine just starts to come to a simmer. Simmer 5 minutes but watch carefully and *do not* let wine come to a boil – boiling will cook away the alcohol and result in a non-alcoholic mulled wine (unless you want a non-alcoholic drink; in which case let it boil the alcohol away). Remove from heat and cover. Let sit an additional 15 minutes to allow flavors to blend. Remove spices and fruit rings. Serve warm. Reheat if necessary but again, do not boil. Garnish glasses or the batch.

Crockpot method:

A crockpot or similar slow cooker is really the ideal way to prepare and serve mulled wine. You can "cook" the wine in the slow cooker and keep it turned to 'warm' or 'low' setting to keep it warm for a party. Simply combine all ingredients except the garnish. Heat on low for one to two hours, then turn to warm to serve. Remove spices and fruit rings. Garnish individual glasses or the pot. Serve warm.

SANGRIA

Sangria is the warm months' answer to mulled wine. Cool, fruity, and delicious, all your summer gatherings should feature pitchers of delicious homemade Sangria made with your delicious homemade wine.

Traditionally made with a dry red wine, there are many, many versions of sangria, including mix-and-match recipes, so you should feel free to experiment to your heart's content. With their fruity and berry bases, almost any country wine is a perfect base for a nice, cool, summer sangria.

It is also traditional for Sangria to include brandy, but often if you are combining two or more types of wine you'll find the brandy extraneous. And of course, you can always leave it off if you prefer. Adding sparkling water or seltzer can also give your punch a nice zip.

- 2 bottles (750 ml; about 2 quarts total) red wine (or your wine preference)
- 1 orange (washed, seeds removed, rind on, cut into slices and halved)
- 1 apple (washed, seeds and core removed, skin on, cut into slices)

- ½ cup sugar (more or less to taste)
- 1 ½ cups orange juice (more or less to taste)
- ¾ cups brandy (more or less to taste)

Combine wine and all liquids in a large (2 quarts+) pitcher. Add sugar and stir until dissolved. Add fruit slices to pitcher and muddle a bit to release some of the juices. Refrigerating for two to four hours will help to further draw and blend the fruit flavors.

Serve cold with ice. If desired, garnish with additional fruit slices.

SIMPLY STUNNING SPARKLING WINE SPRITZERS

Summer is for friends and relaxing with cool drinks, and so it never hurts us to have a second wine cocktail in our arsenal!

These very, very simple wine spritzers can be made by the glass or in a large pitcher for a crowd. Absolutely any wine in your rack will do – use the flavor of your fancy!

All you will need is your wine of choice; plain seltzer, sparkling water, or tonic water; ice; and optional, but recommended, lemon slices (could be lime depending on your wine, or fresh berries or other fruit slices that compliment your wine selection are good selections as well).

Simply place ice in a glass or pint mason jar and pour one part wine over the ice. Add three parts seltzer or another sparkling beverage. (I usually make these in 2-cup mason jars, using ½ cup wine and ¾ cup sparkling water for each.) Top with a slice of lemon or preferred fruit or garnish. Mix gently and enjoy.

CHEERS! TO YOU AND TO EASY WINE MAKING!

The best intentions of this book are to make wine making less intimidating and more accessible for any winemaker looking for a more traditional, less complicated way to make wine. It's wine making taken back to its roots, before all the sulfites and preservatives and additives – which have made wine literally sickening and undrinkable for many people. It's wine making that strives to strip the equipment down to basic, accessible everyday items that don't have to cost a lot. It's wine making with the intention of making making wine *fun*; an interesting hobby affordable enough to experiment, create, and play a little, too.

My hope is that I've made making wine at home a little more approachable for you. There is, truthfully, a world of wine-making information out there, and truthfully, none of it (or very little of it) is "bad" advice; just different. A different approach, one maybe more complex, more designed than another. Which is perfectly *okay*.

What I don't mean to do is make you feel trapped or tied into any one camp or another, be it mine or someone else's. Though I started off with the most basic of information when I started making wine with Mr. Petersohn's scant few lines of instruction, over the decade since I've picked and read and ignored and discarded and embraced small parts of processes, recipes, and advice, and instructions from other home winemakers and experts, too. My process still closely resembles those earliest wines and truth be told I haven't changed a lot, but I have changed some and I've gained some good advice that has improved a recipe here or there or saved a batch I thought might other-wise be a bust.

And this, my friends, is precisely the point. I encourage you, too, to do what feels comfortable for you.

It's so very easy to get caught up in all the information that is out there. As said, it's not that it's bad information; there's just a lot of it and it can be very overwhelming for a start. It can also strip the enjoy-ment out of home winemaking if your intention is to just make a simple, tasty, country wine. So start here. Decide your practice. It's the basis upon which all the other information practices anyway, really, because it is winemaking at its heart. The basic process that is the same root for everyone. Read some more and pick and choose your way through it. Or don't. I don't, for the most part. I keep it simple, manageable, able to fit into my busy home, homesteading, and life. As Frank Petersohn liked to say, *"When you've had a couple of successes (think positive), you may decide to reread one of those "real" books on making wine. This time it may all make a little more sense and not seem as daunting."*

Just never feel like there is only one way. Sure maybe you'll have some failures. I don't believe there is a winemaker out there who has made any appreciable amount of wine who hasn't. You'll notice in the references section that I do reference a lot of these more chemical and additive-based websites and resources. I read them. I refer to them with a question or to troubleshoot a batch. They're good people. I like to learn. But I also disregard a lot of what's being put out there, only because it's not the practice for me. I consider it all, and then land somewhere usually a little aside the middle and more towards the most natural, back-to-basics pathway. Because Grandma knew a lot, lived and thrived and fed her family well, and we've all too often gone too far away from that.

The point is, like most things, our modern science and technology and our advanced understanding of the minutiae of things has taught us a lot; but it's taken us away from a lot of good, wholesome, simple things that we could enjoy a lot more. So form your own practice. Give it a try. Raise a glass and *CHEERS!*

RESOURCES

EQUIPMENT SHOPPING LIST

Basics needed to get started:

- Minimum of 1, 5-gallon food-grade plastic bucket, lid optional
- (2 buckets is recommended for easier straining and transferring)
- 1 package of cheesecloth per batch *OR*
- Plastic wrap *OR*
- Large linen/"flour sack" towels (*recommended)
- 5-gallon plastic water jug *OR* 5-gallon carboy/demijohn per batch (reusable, but each batch will keep the jug in use for at least 1 month)
- Supplies to make airlock:
- Length of tubing (18-24 inches for the airlock)
- Bottle cap or cover (typically comes with the bottle)
- Duct tape
- Glass jar
- *OR*
- 1 Airlock per Carboy/Fermentation jug
- 1 roll of inexpensive duct tape
- Siphoning supplies:

- 4 to 6 feet of food-safe tubing to be used for siphoning **OR**
- Wine-making siphon
- For bottling:
- Wine bottles (about 20 for each 5-gallon batch)
- Screw caps **OR**
- Fresh corks **OR**
- Alternative storage bottles and caps from "additional" list below

Other Recommended Equipment:

- Latex, vinyl, or rubber gloves
- Kitchen food masher

Additional optional equipment to consider:

- 2-3 (or more) buckets if you plan to do a lot of winemaking, or might have more than one batch going at the same time (remember, each batch will stay in this primary fermenter for about a week)
- One or more smaller, 2-3 gallon buckets for smaller batches
- Large rubber bands, large enough to stretch around the outer perimeter of the bucket (for large buckets, elastic trash barrel bands work well;)
- 1 kitchen thermometer for measuring temperature when pitching yeast
- Additional 5-gallon plastic water jugs for additional batches
- Plastic water jugs in various sizes for smaller batches (1-gallon and-3 gallon jugs in addition to the 5-gallon make for a nice, rounded equipment stock)
- Replacement caps for wine storage and racking (optional)
- Balloons if you wish to try the balloon airlock method
- Pin for poking holes
- Corker for corking bottles (needed if storing and capping with corks)
- One or two wine decanters or pitchers for serving

- Alternatives to wine bottles for bottling:
- Mason or canning jars with two-piece lids in good condition
- Swing-top bottles
- Soda bottles with caps
- Other recyclable bottles, jars, or containers (glass preferred, with tight-fitting lids in good condition)

INGREDIENT SHOPPING LIST

1-Gallon Wine Batch

- 4 pounds* of fruit or produce
- 2 pounds* sugar
- 1 packet yeast**

3-Gallon Wine Batch

- 12 pounds* fruit or produce
- 6 pounds* sugar
- 1 packet yeast**

5-Gallon Wine Batch

- 20 pounds* fruit or produce
- 10 pounds* sugar
- 1 packet yeast**

*amounts given are average for basic wine recipes; for more specific quantities, reference "**Chart: Ingredient Amounts for Common Wines**" or specific wine recipes

1 packet yeast for all batch sizes from one to five gallons is correct; for more detailed yeast selection, reference "Chart: Fast-Reference Yeast Selection**"

CHART: INGREDIENT AMOUNTS FOR COMMON WINES

Type of Fruit	# of Pounds	Pounds of Sugar	Amount of Yeast	Approx. Amount Water to Start
Apple	35	8	1 packet	4 gallons
Apricot	18	13	1 packet	4 gallons
Blackberry	18	14	1 packet	4 gallons
Blueberry	12	14	1 packet	4 gallons
Cherries	14	12	1 packet	4 gallons
Chokecherries	13	13	1 packet	4 gallons
Crabapple	26	10	1 packet	4 gallons
Currant	15	13	1 packet	4 gallons
Elderberry	18	12	1 packet	4 gallons
Grapes	18	10	1 packet	4 gallons
Gooseberry	20	12	1 packet	4 gallons
Peach	18	12	1 packet	4 gallons
Pear	20	10	1 packet	4 gallons
Plum	13	12	1 packet	4 gallons
Raspberry	12	13	1 packet	4 gallons
Strawberry	13	8	1 packet	4 gallons

CHART: FAST-REFERENCE YEAST SELECTION

Yeast Name	Fermentation Vigor	Reliability	Temperature Range Tolerance	Produce Partners	Flavor & Aroma Profile	Comparable Commercial Wine Styles	Notes
Bread or Baker's Yeast	Good to Very Good	Moderately High	Good-Normal	All	Neutral under good conditions	N/A	An easy-to-access, cheap, all-around option
Premier Classique (Montrachet)	Very Good	High	Good-Normal	All	Neutral	N/A	Highest recommend-ation of experts; all-purpose; neutral base for any fruit or flavor
Cote des Blanc	Good but Slow	Moderate-Moderately High	Okay-Below normal; more temperature-sensitive	Lighter, whiter fruits, apples	Fruity	Sweeter white wines; Riesling; Chardonnay; Mead	Tends to produce sweeter wines but temperature sensitivity makes it more challenging
Premier Rouge	Very Good	High	Okay-Normal, but low-end sensitive	Wild grapes, Elderberry, Raspberry, Blackberry	Develops flavor of fruit used	Heavy Red Wines; Pinot's, Syrah, Cabernet	Reliable; helps bring out more subtle fruit flavors and weak and/or sub-optimally ripened fruits
Premier Blanc	Very Good	High	Very good-Above Normal; High-end temp range friendly	Lighter fruits; apples; meads	Neutral	Dry White Wines and Dry Ciders; Sauvignon Blanc	A more reliable yeast for white wine production but produces dryer, less sweet white wines
K1-V1116	Very Good	High	Very good-Above Normal	Fresh fruits, juice concentrates, peaches,	Neutral, fresh; develops flavors of fruit used	Sauvignon Blanc, Chenin Blanc	Performs well in low-nutrient environments; good base for developing

							light fruit flavors
RC-212	Good	Moderate	Good-Normal	Dark grapes and dark berries	Ripe berry, spice, pepper	Burgundy, Pinot Noir, Full-bodied Red wines	Known for full flavor extraction and making the most of all that a fruit can give
EC-1118	Very Good	High	Very good-Above Normal	All fruits; late-harvest fruits; ice wine fruits	Neutral	Champagne and Sparkling wines; Red or white wines	Lalvin's all-purpose yeast; usable for both red and white wine styles; a good yeast for stuck fermentation; good when environment and temperature conditions are unreliable

HELPFUL EQUIVALENTS & CONVERSIONS

- 1 pound sugar = approx. 2 cups

Helpful metric conversions:

- 5 gallons = 18.9 liters
- 1 quart = .95 liter
- 1 pound = .45 Kg

Easier estimated quick-conversion amounts:

- 5 gallons = 20 liters
- 1 quart = 1 liter
- 2 pounds = 1 Kg

STEP-BY-STEP WINE MAKING PROCESS REVIEW

Following is a fast summary of the wine-making process, provided as a quick reference. If you need more detail on any step, see detailed instructions in Chapter 4.

Day Before or Day One:

1. Gather and clean your equipment.

Equipment needed for primary fermentation: Colanders, gloves (optional, recommended), 5-gallon bucket, mashing utensils/equipment, large stockpot, misc. kitchen equipment

To sterilize: 1 tablespoon bleach per gallon of water, or solution of 16 Campden tablets per gallon of water plus ½ teaspoon citric acid per gallon

Day One:

2. Gather and prep fruit or produce.

Wash and drain fruit. (To clean with vinegar use 1 part vinegar to 3 parts water.)

De-stem, de-seed (if possible or practical) or de-pit.

Cut or crush into mash or pieces for must

3. Make the fruit must.

Crush, squeeze, mash, or process soft fruits, berries, and grapes. Cut larger fruits like apples, pears, and stone fruits into small chunks. Work in batches so that all berries/fruits are broken and juice is extracted. Dump the must into your fermenting bucket.

4. Dissolve sugar in water.

**Note: You may choose to do this before you start crushing or cutting the fruit for the must. This allows the sugar-water to cool before adding it to the fruit juice and must, or more importantly, before pitching the yeast.

Simmer the sugar in enough water to dissolve it (about 2 gallons for a 5-gallon wine batch), but do not use all the water that the recipe calls for (to ensure you have enough room in the fermenter later). Stir occasionally as you heat.

5. Combine sugar-water and fruit must.

Mix together in fermenting bucket.

6. Top with water.

Add water to the juice/must but do not fill bucket all the way. Leave 4 to 5 inches at the top so that the cap has room to rise during fermentation. (Cool or cold water is fine to add if you need to cool down the must).

7. Prep & pitch the yeast.

Take about 2 cups of must and water mix. Add a little water to make it fluid, if necessary. Check the temperature of the must and make sure it's not too hot – not more than 105°F. Sprinkle yeast over top. Rehydrate 15 minutes. Stir in and let foam 15 minutes more. Check temperature of must in bucket. Pitch yeast when must is around 85°F. Stir.

8. Set for primary fermentation.

Place bucket in warm (around 70°F), draft-free area and cover lightly with clean linen cloth. Let ferment for one week. Stir daily.

Day 7:

9. Strain must.

Strain off all the solids (the fruit must/mash), reserving the liquid (the wine).

10. Rack for secondary fermentation.

Using a funnel, pour wine into secondary fermenting jug/carboy/demijohn. Fit tightly with air-tight airlock system. Place in fermenting area. Let ferment for about one month until wine clears of hazy solids and sediment layer forms on the bottom.

Week 4:

11. Siphon, rack or bottle.

After secondary fermentation completes, siphon the clear wine from above the sediment layer. If racking for a third time, transfer to clean fermenting jug/carboy/demijohn. Eliminate headspace (airspace) if necessary to avoid spoilage and air exposure. Bottle when wine is clear and free of sediment (*if racking a second time, bottle around **Week 8 to 10**).

12. Age.

Age bottled wine for desired period of time. Wine is safe to drink after completed secondary fermentation. Aging period of three to six months is recommended for most wines.

Week 12+:

13. ENJOY!

Cheers!!

REFERENCES & INTERESTING RECOMMENDED READING

The Fantastic, Fabled Frank Petersohn:

"How To Make Wine In No Time, The Cheap Way ." *Ingeb.org.* **N. p., 2019. Web. 19 July 2019.**

"Adjust Wine Flavor In The Fermenter - Winemakermag.Com." *Wine-MakerMag.com.* N. p., 2019. Web. 2 Aug. 2019.

"Are There Adverse Effects To Adding Diammonium Phosphate (DAP) As A Yeast Nutrient In Red Wine? | Wine Spectator." *Wine Spectator.* N. p., 2019. Web. 2 Aug. 2019.

"Beet Wine - My First Attempt." *Wine Making Talk.* N. p., 2019. Web. 31 July 2019.

Books, Our et al. "Homemade Mead: A Honey Mead Recipe With Flavoring Suggestions." *DIY Natural.* N. p., 2018. Web. 2 Aug. 2019.

"Bottling, Start To Finish - Winemakermag.Com." *WineMakerMag.com.* N. p., 2019. Web. 2 Aug. 2019.

"Campden Tablet Uses ." *Winemakersdepot.com.* N. p., 2019. Web. 2 Aug. 2019.

"Can I Make A Sulfite-Free Wine? - Winemakermag.Com." *WineMaker-Mag.com*. N. p., 2019. Web. 2 Aug. 2019.

"Choosing A Wine Yeast Strain - Winemakermag.Com." *WineMaker-Mag.com*. N. p., 2019. Web. 2 Aug. 2019.

Connelly, Andy. "The Science And Magic Of Wine-Making | Andy Connelly." *the Guardian*. N. p., 2013. Web. 31 July 2019.

"Country Wine Yeast: Tips From The Pros - Winemakermag.Com." *WineMakerMag.com*. N. p., 2019. Web. 2 Aug. 2019.

"Elderflower Wine Recipe - Light To Medium Bodied." *Home Brew Answers*. N. p., 2017. Web. 2 Aug. 2019.

"Five Wine Making Fundamentals." *Eckraus.com*. N. p., 2019. Web. 31 July 2019.

Frazer, Jennifer. "Wine Becomes More Like Whisky As Alcohol Content Gets High." *Scientific American*. N. p., 2014. Web. 2 Aug. 2019.

"Frequently Asked Questions | Midwest Supplies." *Midwestsupplies.com*. N. p., 2019. Web. 2 Aug. 2019.

"Home - And Here We Are." *And Here We Are*. N. p., 2019. Web. 2 Aug. 2019.

Homebrewit.com. N. p., 2019. Web. 2 Aug. 2019.

"Home - Home Brew Answers." *Home Brew Answers*. N. p., 2019. Web. 2 Aug. 2019.

"Home - Lallemand Brewing." *Lallemandbrewing.com*. N. p., 2019. Web. 2 Aug. 2019.

"How Long Are Yeast Packets Good For?." *Wine Making Talk*. N. p., 2019. Web. 2 Aug. 2019.

"How To Detect A Stuck Fermentation." *Winemaker's Academy*. N. p., 2014. Web. 2 Aug. 2019.

"How To Know When To Rack Your Wine." *Winemaker's Academy*. N. p., 2013. Web. 2 Aug. 2019.

"How To Make Tomato Wine From Homegrown Tomatoes." *Sow True Seed*. N. p., 2019. Web. 2 Aug. 2019.

"How To Stop Fermentation." *Eckraus.com*. N. p., 2019. Web. 31 July 2019.

"Is Headspace In Carboy Bad?." *Wine Making Talk*. N. p., 2019. Web. 2 Aug. 2019.

"Jay's Brewing - Northern VA's Longest Standing Brewing Supply Store.." *Jaysbrewing.com*. N. p., 2019. Web. 2 Aug. 2019.

Kiley, Christie. "Why You Need A Hydrometer When Making Wine." *WineCoolerDirect.com*. N. p., 2014. Web. 2 Aug. 2019.

Kraus, Ed. "Are All Wine Yeast The Same? | E. C. Kraus Wine Making." *Wine Making and Beer Brewing Blog | EC Kraus*. N. p., 2013. Web. 31 July 2019.

Kraus, Ed. "A Simple Guide To Choosing Wine Yeast | E. Kraus." *Wine Making and Beer Brewing Blog | EC Kraus*. N. p., 2018. Web. 2 Aug. 2019.

Kraus, Ed. "Bulk Storing Wine In A Carboy | E. C. Kraus Wine Making." *Wine Making and Beer Brewing Blog | EC Kraus*. N. p., 2018. Web. 2 Aug. 2019.

Kraus, Ed. "How Do I Know When A Wine Fermentation Is Done?." *Wine Making and Beer Brewing Blog | EC Kraus*. N. p., 2016. Web. 2 Aug. 2019.

Kraus, Ed. "How Much Wine Yeast To Use? | E. C. Kraus Wine Making." *Wine Making and Beer Brewing Blog | EC Kraus*. N. p., 2019. Web. 31 July 2019.

Kraus, Ed. "I Have Too Much Headspace In The Secondary Fermenter." *Wine Making and Beer Brewing Blog | EC Kraus*. N. p., 2018. Web. 2 Aug. 2019.

Kraus, Ed. "Increasing Your Wine's Fruity Flavors | E. C. Kraus Wine-making." *Wine Making and Beer Brewing Blog | EC Kraus*. N. p., 2018. Web. 2 Aug. 2019.

Kraus, Ed. "Making Wine With Bread Yeast... Not | E. C. Kraus Wine Making." *Wine Making and Beer Brewing Blog | EC Kraus*. N. p., 2017. Web. 2 Aug. 2019.

Kraus, Ed. "My Wine's Fermenting Without Adding Any Yeast | E. C. Kraus." *Wine Making and Beer Brewing Blog | EC Kraus*. N. p., 2018. Web. 31 July 2019.Kraus, Ed. "3 Tips To Make Fruit Wine With More Fruit Flavor." *Wine Making and Beer Brewing Blog | EC Kraus*. N. p., 2018. Web. 31 July 2019.

"Lees (Fermentation)." *En.wikipedia.org*. N. p., 2019. Web. 2 Aug. 2019.

"Mead." *En.wikipedia.org*. N. p., 2018. Web. 2 Aug. 2019.

Motherearthnews.com. N. p., 2019. Web. 2 Aug. 2019.

"Northeast Winemaking - Everything You Need To Make Wine At Home.." *Northeast Winemaking*. N. p., 2019. Web. 2 Aug. 2019.

"NPR Choice Page." *Npr.org*. N. p., 2019. Web. 2 Aug. 2019.

"Ph Testing | Morewine." *Morewinemaking.com*. N. p., 2019. Web. 2 Aug. 2019.

Postmodernwinemaking.com. N. p., 2019. Web. 2 Aug. 2019.

"Racking Wine." *Eckraus.com*. N. p., 2019. Web. 2 Aug. 2019.

"Shelf Life And Storage: Dry Yeast | Red Star Yeast." *Redstaryeast.com*. N. p., 2019. Web. 2 Aug. 2019.

"Should I Wash Fresh Fruit In Vinegar? | Bestfoodfacts.Org." *Best Food Facts*. N. p., 2018. Web. 2 Aug. 2019.

"Simplifying Cleaning And Sanitizing For Home Winemakers." *Bader Beer & Wine Supply*. N. p., 2017. Web. 2 Aug. 2019.

"Take Control Of Must Temperature-And Reap The Benefits - Winemakermag.Com." *WineMakerMag.com*. N. p., 2019. Web. 31 July 2019.

Temperature, Drinking. "Ideal Wine Room Temperature - Wine Guardian® Cooling Units." *Wine Guardian®: Wine Cellar Cooling Units*. N. p., 2018. Web. 2 Aug. 2019.

"Testing The Must For Sugar Content, PH, And TA | Morewine." *Morewinemaking.com*. N. p., 2019. Web. 2 Aug. 2019.

"The Winemaking Home Page." *Winemaking.jackkeller.net*. N. p., 2019. Web. 2 Aug. 2019.

Three Ways To Melomel." *AleHorn - Viking Drinking Horn Vessels and Accessories*. N. p., 2019. Web. 2 Aug. 2019.

Ucfoodsafety.ucdavis.edu. N. p., 2019. Web. 2 Aug. 2019.

"Using Fruit Extract To Enhance Flavor." *Wine Making Talk*. N. p., 2019. Web. 2 Aug. 2019.

"What Do "Ph" And "TA" Numbers Mean To A Wine? | Wine Spectator." *Wine Spectator*. N. p., 2019. Web. 2 Aug. 2019.

"What, Exactly, IS Yeast Nutrient?." *Craft Beer & Brewing*. N. p., 2019. Web. 2 Aug. 2019.

"What Is The Shelf Life For Dry Yeast? Is There Anything I Can Do To Revive It And Will It Work? - Winemakermag.Com." *WineMakerMag.com*. N. p., 2019. Web. 2 Aug. 2019.

"What Is Yeast? | Singer Instruments." *Singerinstruments.com*. N. p., 2019. Web. 31 July 2019."Wine Recipes | Home Wine Making | EC Kraus." *Eckraus.com*. N. p., 2019. Web. 31 July 2019.

"What Yeasts Make Fruit Wine | Midwest Supplies." *Midwestsupplies.com*. N. p., 2019. Web. 2 Aug. 2019.

"When Is My Wine Fermentation Finished?." *Homebrewing Learn Center*. N. p., 2016. Web. 2 Aug. 2019.

"When Should I Bottle My Wine? - Keystone Homebrew Supply." *Keystone Homebrew Supply*. N. p., 2010. Web. 2 Aug. 2019.

"Wine Bottle Storage And Temperature." *Eckraus.com*. N. p., 2019. Web. 31 July 2019.

"Wine Fermentation 101." *Eckraus.com*. N. p., 2019. Web. 31 July 2019.

"Wine Making Supplies & Brewing Supplies | Homebrewit.Com :: Homebrewit.Com." *Homebrewit.com*. N. p., 2019. Web. 2 Aug. 2019.

"Winemaking: Wild Plum Wines." *Winemaking.jackkeller.net*. N. p., 2019. Web. 2 Aug. 2019.

"Winemaking: Wine Problems." *Winemaking.jackkeller.net*. N. p., 2019. Web. 2 Aug. 2019.

"7 Wine-Storage Basics You Need To Know | Wine Spectator." *Wine Spectator*. N. p., 2019. Web. 2 Aug. 2019.

"Yeast Fundamentals | Wyeast Laboratories." *Wyeastlab.com*. N. p., 2019. Web. 2 Aug. 2019.

"Yeast Too Old." *Eckraus.com*. N. p., 2019. Web. 2 Aug. 2019.

"Yeast In Winemaking." *En.wikipedia.org*. N. p., 2019. Web. 31 July 2019.

"Yeast Strain Chart - Distillers Wiki." *Homedistiller.org*. N. p., 2019. Web. 2 Aug. 2019.

ABOUT THE AUTHOR

Homesteading, house-holding, farming, gardening, being a wife and mother, and yes, writing, too, represent the majority of ways Mary Ellen Ward spends her days. Believing in living well and days that end in a feeling of accomplishment, finding ways to incorporate some of the most valuable old-school ways of life into a busy modern one is what she truly enjoys. Mary considers herself highly fortunate to be able to do so, and enjoys sharing her knowledge and experiences with others who are similarly inclined. Look for other titles from Mary Ellen Ward, both past and future.

❧

From easy stand mixer bread recipes to cleaner prep-ahead mixes, you can find more homesteading and related titles by Mary Ellen Ward on Amazon.com. Visit her Author Page where you can find a list of all current, new, and upcoming releases by Mary. Be a part of Mary's community of followers and check out pictures she shares, blog posts and updates, important links, and her biography.

THE HOMEMADE HOMESTEAD

You can also find Mary Ellen Ward sharing her life, tips, tricks, current projects, and other books and resources at her website, TheHomemadeHomestead.com. To be easily updated with new posts, please subscribe to The Homemade Homestead.

SPECIAL THANKS

Many thanks are owed to many people—plenty of family and friends who have selflessly supported my wine-making endeavors over the years (you poor, poor souls…somebody's got to do it). However, special thanks are owed to Mrs. Mary Barclay for support, encouragement, and editorial assistance.
Many Thanks, Mary, from "Me"!

Thanks are owed also to Frank Petersohn's son, Michael, who generously granted his permission to quote and paraphrase Frank's works. Michael also gave generously of his own time to answer various questions that I had as best he could, delving deep into Frank's email archives to share his father's knowledge and insights. I am grateful also for the stories and anecdotes Michael shared with me of his father, and of the memories he had of his father's love of simple winemaking. His hope, like mine, is that this book makes this enjoyable hobby more approachable for others, in honor of Frank and the hobby he devoted so much of his time to sharing.
Many, many Thanks, Michael!

Special Thanks

~ If you have enjoyed this book and / or found any small part of it useful, your honest review would be very much appreciated, by both the author and fellow and future readers.
Thoughtful reviews help good books to be found! ~
Thank You!

DISCLAIMER

The safety and success of wines made at home or in any other venues depend on many factors, including, but not limited to: Sanitation practices, preparation and procedures used and followed throughout all stages of wine making, ingredient safety and cleanliness, alcohol content of the wine and other factors, care and storage of wine, ingredients, and equipment, many related and additional practices, procedures, and processes. As such, neither the author, publisher, nor any person or entity mentioned in this book can be held liable for the outcome, associated costs, or health and safety of products produced from information contained in this book, nor can they be held liable for illness or injury that may occur as the result of any product, process, method, ingredient, information, or suggestion contained herein. Care and safe, sanitary cooking practices must always be observed. This book is presented for informational purposes only and by reading and using this book you agree that the author, publisher, and persons named herein can in no way be held liable for any resulting illness, loss, or injury. Use at your own risk.

NOTES

NOTES

NOTES

NOTES

Printed in Great Britain
by Amazon

85775452R00180